T0267702

the PEACE *of* REIKI

Practices for Co-Creating New Earth

Anya Light

IN PRAISE OF
THE PEACE OF REIKI

Anya has written a wonderful book, which is an exploration of the inner state of mind needed to practice the system of Reiki and to lead a life of love and compassion. Or as she says: to create New Earth. This is so important, especially at this time in our current world situation.

—Frans Stiene, founder of the International House of Reiki and author of *The Way of Reiki*, *The Inner Heart of Reiki*, and *Reiki Insights*

The Peace of Reiki is a thorough instructor's manual, new student guidebook, and Reiki Guru companion. Anya Light covers the gamut of Reiki, intimately discussing practicality, practice, and integration to make for a more peaceful practitioner. Her writing is charming and insightful as she shares personal discoveries of the New Earth and practice invitations to guide the readers into incorporating Reiki into each and every moment.

—Halina Schriefer, founder of Ordinary Pioneer Community (ordinarypioneer.com)

The Peace of Reiki is an invitation to open your heart and a gentle, oh-so-loving reminder to live our Reiki, to simply be Reiki. Anya's heartfelt passion and love pour out of every page. Whether you are just beginning your Reiki journey or are a Master, this book will meet you exactly where you are. You'll learn powerful self-healing techniques that you can use daily and share with others. I will return to these words of wisdom again and again as I incorporate its lessons into my own teachings and life. Grab a cup of tea, sip it slow, and open this book as we awaken New Earth together. I recommend this book with all of my heart.

—Katy Mercer, founder of The Lavender Hour Community (thelavenderhour.com)

This beautiful work, *The Peace of Reiki*, sits comfortably atop the most intuitive works on the subject I have read. Through a practical and personal understanding of Reiki, Anya brings the comfort of her knowing into the reader's being.

—Narus Janus Sandas, creator of *The Wisdom of the Crow Tarot*

This book is dedicated to Halina:
Soul Sister,
New Earth Builder,
Divine Mother to us all

TABLE OF CONTENTS

THANKS

The creation of this book was a perfect symphony of hearts. It is with deep gratitude that I bow to the following individuals who offered so freely of their time, energy, and love.

Deepest thanks to my soul sister Halina Schriefer, whose insightful eye gazed upon every single one of these pages. I could not have asked for a more wonderful editor or a more amazing friend on the path. *~Thank you for the clarity of your vision & the grace of your Spirit, dearest Halina.*

Sending love and gratitude to the beautiful Katy Mercer, who, despite being "biscuits busy," was always available to read chapters and offer an encouraging, enthusiastic word. *~ Sister, you lifted me up at a point on the journey when I needed you most. Many Thanks! I Love You!*

Finally, boundless blessings to my Ordinary Pioneer family for their support and to all the friends who shared insights on individual chapters. Special thanks to: Gabriel, Kim High, Ian Colin McCain, Linzi Jenkins, Kim Simon, Brittani Bellfy, Chad Premo, Paul Narus Sandas, Kristi Marie Fuller, Kevin Fuller, Carole Sarkan, Roman Vaynshtok, Shay Ferguson, Meg Cekada Thomas, Kayla Harris, Mandy Bird, Michael Ellison, Roseann Wintringham, Mary Jean Gill DeRousie, Linette Mitchell Will, and Jennifer Featherston.

AN INVITATION TO PATIENCE

Over the years, Reiki becomes us. We must be patient for its unfolding. It is not something to be grasped overnight.

Indeed, as with all great blessings, the practice of Reiki takes time. It's a *process*. It's a mysterious dance of events and visions that lead us to precisely where we need to be.

To begin this book, I invite you—in the spirit of patience—to close your eyes and take a deep breath…right now…

…Thank you!

Did you know that your willingness to stop and breathe is—quite literally—the essence of Reiki?

Yes!!

Reiki is the glorious permission to pause. A daring moment of Peace.

INTRODUCTION

When practiced diligently, Reiki becomes the flower of our life. Its petals unfold with magnificent precision.

Whether we pursue Masters-level training or are content with *Shoden* (Level One), the lessons we learn on the Reiki path have the potential to uplift every single moment of our daily life. For indeed, Reiki is not merely the pursuit of physical health—it is an all-encompassing road to world peace! It is a way for human beings to live harmoniously upon Planet Earth!

Perhaps you've recently received your first attunement. Or perhaps you've read books about energy healing or received a Reiki healing session. Or perhaps you've been teaching Reiki for many years and are ready to journey deeper. Wherever you are on the path, I welcome you. This book is for you.

Some Reading Suggestions

There are 21 chapters in this book. My choice of 21 is intentional: it's a bow to Mikao Usui, the founder of Reiki. During his 21-day fast on Mount Kurama, he underwent a radical transformation. As he merged into the pure Reiki Light beyond name and form, he obtained Enlightenment—and not just for himself, but as a promise for all beings. Thus, the sacred number 21, mentioned throughout this text, is a blessing for you, from him.

As you read this book, please know that there is no particular order in which you must read. Each chapter may stand alone. In other words, the insights presented in this book are not meant to be linear or progressive. For example, practice number 8 is not more advanced than practice number 3. As such, key concepts and practices will be explained multiple times from multiple angles. This repetition is intentional. For most of us, it is necessary to hear the *dharma*—the true nature of reality—again and again and again. Truth takes time to sink in.

Please approach this book as a living oracle. If you're feeling unmotivated to practice or feeling confused about your life, take a breath and open the book to a 'random' page. There you will find answers to your questions and feel a fresh burst of inspiration in your heart.

I also recommend that you take your sweet time. If a particular practice or chapter feels extra nourishing for you, please resist the temptation to read further. Pause. Relax. Breathe. Let it all sink in. If it takes you many years to fully traverse these pages, that's absolutely wonderful! There's no need to rush.

While anybody who has an interest in energy work can benefit from this book, *The Peace of Reiki* has been specifically designed to guide those who have been personally trained by a Reiki teacher. Thus, if you occasionally read something that's beyond your current level of understanding, please don't worry. If any concept or tool is unclear (such as my discussions about the symbols or mantras, for example), please feel free to skip that chapter and focus instead on the other chapters that already make sense to you.

Please also be aware: My words may not always resonate with you. Each one of us has unique conditioning that draws us to certain words, and repels us from others. Sometimes I may use the word "God." Sometimes I may use the words "Divinity" or "Consciousness" or "Universe." While all of these words may sing to my Soul, perhaps you feel differently. Therefore, at any point during the reading, if you find yourself irritated, then I invite you to simply substitute the undesired word for one that suits you better. Ultimately, words are simply pointers, helping us to tap into realities that are beyond the conceptual mind.

Experiencing Reiki

In the following chapters, I'll offer you guidance in both the philosophy and practice of Reiki. While philosophy is of course vitally important, I do recommend that you place a greater bulk of your attention on my Practice Invitations. These appear at the end of each chapter.

To find peace, one must go beyond mere thoughts, ideas and concepts. One must be willing to go through the purifying fires of daily practice in order to truly *embody* that peace.

Indeed, to co-create peaceful, harmonious relationships, one must—at a certain point—move beyond merely theorizing. One must be willing to go through challenging tests and trials—to get one's hands messy in the emotional muck of daily life.

I invite your curious investigation. Verify through your own experience if what I'm saying is true.

And remember...honor your own intuition above all else!

The Story of 'Me'

I was born in the state of Michigan in the United States of America. My parents gave me the name Heather McMacken. I grew up in middle-class suburbs, absorbing the values of a strict Presbyterian household. My grandfather was a minister. Christian values were embedded into my consciousness from the very first days.

Although everything about my life probably looked lovely to outside eyes, there were darker truths afoot. I had an extremely challenging childhood. A cascade of abusive, neglectful, traumatic events happened, causing a deep scar upon my soul. My teenage years and early adulthood were a fog of depression, Complex PTSD, addictions, and a variety of chronic illnesses that no doctor could seem to fix. Therapists and self-help books didn't help much. By my late twenties, I'd had enough. I wanted to die.

Despite the overwhelming darkness, however, I somehow managed to move to Ohio and earn a Ph.D. in English. My poems got published and I received some acclaim. Like the singer-songwriter Leonard Cohen (one of my heroes), I somehow spun shadows into light. I turned my tragedy into art.

It was in the midst of this artistic period that Reiki found me. Somehow, I ended up on a massage table, with Reiki Hands on my forehead. It felt as if the weight of the world was finally being lifted from my body!! It was a miracle!! For the first time in my life, I felt hope.

Between the ages of 28 and 29, I completed my Reiki training. My wonderful teacher Barb Hay, a visionary painter and poet, was not only my mentor, but also my dear friend. We loved co-teaching Reiki classes as much as we loved simply hanging out, giggling over steaming cups of coffee.

Shortly after I completed my training with Barb, she relocated to Chicago. I remained in Ohio and began to teach Reiki on my own. It was intense and awesome! I got deeper into spirituality and published a book called *Opening Love*. I began to receive interview invitations and requests to speak at festivals, churches, and conferences. A natural introvert, every bone in my body wanted to flee! However, I kept on saying *yes*. I knew this was God's plan for me.

A few years later, I changed my name to Anya, which in Sanskrit means "inexhaustible." Indeed, I had an inexhaustible passion for transmitting the blessed teachings of Reiki. This was no longer merely a hobby for me. This was now a full-blown calling: a life mission.

Fast forward ten years to the present day. My physical and mental health are good and constantly improving. When once I struggled to get out of bed, now I have the energy for pilgrimages to India and road trips to sacred sites across the country. When once I felt lethargic and lacked purpose, now I co-create festivals and healing circles with two beautiful Reiki Masters, Halina and Katy, my former apprentices who carry on our lineage. When once I felt bitterness, now I am overflowing with gratitude, relishing acts of *seva* (sacred service) in my role as Spiritual Director at Ordinary Pioneer, a spiritual healing community. Overall, I feel I'm exactly where I need to be. God is making very good use of me!

And, dear reader, it's important that I be real with you. My health—at the time of this writing—is still not quite where I'd like it to be. I'm still working through some remaining physical issues as well as some lingering emotional triggers. This has been an extremely humbling process! Right now, I am learning to accept public leadership while *also* practicing vulnerability and authenticity. Sometimes it's a tightrope. I am learning patience and trust.

As I move through these challenges, I am so so grateful to inspire the work of other wounded healers, people who have also endured great amounts of trauma and illness in their lives. I love reminding them that we do *not* have to be perfect in order to be helpful. We do *not* have to be perfect in order to Love.

Co-Creating New Earth

Around one hundred years ago, the following words were inscribed on Mikao Usui's memorial stone in Tokyo: "If Reiki can be spread throughout the world it will touch the human heart and the morals of society. It will be helpful for many people, and will not only heal disease, but also the Earth as a whole."[1]

Indeed!! Yes!!

Blessedly, what Usui hoped for is happening *now*! Reiki is travelling at lightening-speed across our globe. Countless souls are waking up. This truly is the beginning of a golden age.

Old Earth is dying; New Earth is being born.

Peace is dawning—right now.

Through the blessed path of Reiki, as well as through countless other beautiful paths and traditions, we are remembering the truth of our Oneness. We are dropping our weapons and our worry. We are integrating the (seemingly opposite) dimensions of form and form-lessness. We are bringing in ancient wisdom in new ways. We are merging love and courage.

We are creating this New Earth—together.

---

1 This quote is from one of Usui's direct students and was first translated into English by Frank Arjava Petter in his book *Reiki Fire* (Lotus Light, 1997).

Blessing

The logic of the words I share here are far less important than the energetic transmission you receive. So, in other words, don't get stuck in my ideas. Rather, *feel what happens inside of you as you read.*

For indeed, from the moment you've opened this book, a flowing of Reiki has come.

All you need to do right now is to open your Heart and receive.

CHAPTER 1

THE FIRST PRECEPT: BUILDING TRUST

The whole system of Reiki

is based on embodying the precepts

within oneself and one's life,

not just about hands-on healing for others;

the true aim of the system of Reiki

is about rediscovering our True Self

or enlightenment.

FRANS STIENE

What holds this Universe together? What's the special glue? Some think it's Christ, some think it's Krishna, others think the Buddha makes the world go 'round.

The beautiful thing about the path of Reiki is that we get to *choose*. We are free to gravitate to the story that most resonates. We are free to revere a deity—or not. We are free to study holy scriptures—or not. We are free to trust what our Soul tells us is truth. Indeed, the system of Reiki is compatible with all religions, all worldviews, all cultures, and all walks of life. Nobody is excluded. You can be a dedicated Reiki practitioner and also be very logical and scientific. You can practice Reiki daily and also be a Christian. You can worship as a Muslim or a Hindu. You can be atheist. You can be whatever. All are welcome.

Because Reiki is such a flexible path, it will be—and already is—a major catalyst for the co-creation of New Earth. The system of Reiki reminds us of the healing powers of tolerance and non-judgment. By respecting *all* traditions as beautiful and equally valid, human beings can finally come together, peacefully, as One Family. We can finally come together as a worldwide sacred *sangha* (spiritual community), honoring all ways and paths as unique roads to Divinity.

Part of the Reiki journey is learning to craft, create, and listen to the story that most wants to be told through us. The journey is about hearing how we may contribute uniquely to the whole, while respecting the unique journey of others. It's about honoring our special relationship to the Divine.

Indeed, the relationship we have with Divinity is the most sacred relationship of our life. It's *the* glue. It shapes and colors everything we touch. It gets us out of bed in the morning and brings us courage in times of terror. Consolation in times of grief. Indeed, the story we tell ourselves about how the Universe works is the way we drop into Peace when nothing else works.

We can strengthen this story-relationship by diligently practicing the first Reiki precept: "Just for today, do not worry."

In translations from Japanese into English, this precept is often listed as second. However, I have always intuitively felt that this precept needs to be listed first, for it is truly the most vital, the most crucial for our daily wellbeing.

By healing our tendency to worry, we settle into a life of Peace.

By making our minds calm and free from worry, we can truly embody compassion.

With the help of this precept, we become like angels, rising above the ancient, animalistic patterns of fear and conflict.

With less and less worry, we live a *dharmic* existence, one that is aligned with the True Nature of the Universe.

So, how do we actually live this first precept? How do we stop worry? When confusions or challenges happen in our lives, how do we find Peace?

Whether we revere Allah or Yahweh, whether we bow in prayer to Lakshmi or Quan Yin, whether we find comfort within the scientific method or the natural patterns found in Taoism, it *is* possible to progressively build our trust in Divinity. We can come to trust, no matter what, that Divinity will shelter us.

In truth, every perceived setback, trial, and moment of loss is *not* a mistake. Rather, every single one of these challenging moments is an opportunity to cultivate a deeper relationship with the Divine. Every challenge gives us a gift: We can root like a tree, standing tall in full faith and trust—no matter the winds of change.

Practice Invitation

The next time your mind is lost in worry, please use the following mantra as a powerful antidote:

"I trust in you, _____." (Select a word/name that brings a sense of peace to your heart, such as an enlightened master, higher power, or benevolent force.)

For example, a few of my favorites are:

"I trust in you, Universe"

"I trust in you, Krishna."

"I trust in you, God."

Repeat this mantra continually during times of worry. It's a simple, practical, powerful way to practice the first Reiki precept.

It's also wonderful to incorporate this mantra into your Reiki self-healing sessions. With one hand on your root chakra (genital area) and another hand resting upon your sacral chakra (an inch or two below your belly button), whisper this mantra as you recline on a bed or couch. Snuggle under some cozy blankets and have a cup of warm tea nearby.

Allow yourself to feel protected and cocooned. Allow all worries to dissolve.

CHAPTER 2

THE SECOND PRECEPT & THE SECOND SYMBOL

Just for today, do not anger.

MIKAO USUI

What is anger?

There are many things we could say about anger.

Anger is a fiery uprising.

Anger is a powerful burst of heat.

Anger is a protest.

Ultimately, anger is a moment of blame. Anger says: "Hey Universe, I know what's best—and this should NOT be happening! You're making a HUGE mistake!"

Yes, there are many things we could say about anger. Perhaps the most important, though, is this: Anger is not wrong to feel. Anger is simply a normal human emotion.

We Reiki healers tend to feel ashamed—even sometimes horrified—when anger arises within us. How is it possible to feel such darkness when we've committed our lives to the Light?

Dear friend, I invite you to put this question to rest and to be gentle with yourself whenever anger arises. We don't need to feel ashamed or horrified when we get angry. There is no need to pile darkness on top of darkness!

Dear friend, when anger comes up, we can give ourselves the gift of compassion. We can choose to peel back the layers of anger and recognize what it *actually is*. We can look carefully, noticing the pain of other repressed emotions hiding underneath.

Indeed, if we look beneath the fires of anger, what we'll see are the murky waters of fear, grief, sadness, confusion, and doubt. What we'll see is hidden trauma.

Kindness is so important right now!

The second Reiki precept "Just for today, do not anger" is often misunderstood. Contrary to popular belief, Usui was *not* teaching that we should never feel the emotion of anger. Feeling it is perfectly okay. What's *not* okay, however, is when we project that anger outward onto others with harsh words and deeds. It's *not* okay to hurt people when we're feeling angry.

When I teach the second precept in my classes, I usually add a phrase to help make this precept more clear:

Just for today, do not *act from a place of* anger.

If we remember the precept in this way, we'll remember what to do... In the face of a fiery storm: simply stop. Breathe. Take time to heal.

Yes, anger is *not* a time to take worldly action or to engage with others. (If we do, we'll likely feel regret later.) This precept is a reminder

14

to go inward. Whether it takes us a few seconds or a few minutes or a few hours, it's imperative that we Stop—now.

To help us calm down, we can pair this precept with the second Reiki symbol-mantra, the *Sei Heiki*. (I'll share some practice ideas below.) These linked tools remind us to pause, relax, and "remember our True Self."[2]

For indeed, whenever we are out of balance, it's (ultimately) because we're forgetting our Divinity. And whenever we forget our Divinity, we walk around this world making huge messes! Therefore, we can view the arising of anger as a blessing in disguise—prompting us to take some much-needed downtime.

No, anger is not our enemy. It's simply a reminder to breathe and realign.

Practice Invitation #1

The next time anger arises, take a moment and place your hand over your heart. Begin speaking to the inner child who lives inside.

Whisper that you love them and that it's okay to feel what they're feeling. Share nurturing, supportive words such as:

- "It's okay to feel angry."
- "It makes sense that you're feeling anger right now."
- "It's normal that you feel frustrated. Human life is hard."
- "You're safe with me, dear. Let's heal together."
- "I'm here for you."
- "I fully support you and love you, just as you are."

---

2 This quote is from Frans Stiene's brilliant book *The Inner Heart of Reiki* (page 183). I recommend this book to all my Reiki students.

By giving your inner child permission to feel exactly how they feel, relief will spread throughout your whole being. As the words continue or fade away into a peaceful silence, channel the Reiki energy as needed. Be open to the deeper layers of emotion (such as sadness, fear, or doubt) that may want to arise. Be present with whatever comes. You are safe to feel all of this. You are healing.

Practice Invitation #2

Whenever you feel anger, stop whatever you are doing as soon as possible. Remove yourself from any social situation that you may be in, go home, turn off the phone, close the curtains, and relax peacefully in bed.

While your body becomes heavy, drifting between states of waking and sleeping, repeatedly draw the Sei Heiki symbol in your mind. (If you're unfamiliar with this symbol, that's okay. Simply perform Reiki self-healing while incorporating the next step.)

Visualize that old, toxic layers of pain and trauma are shedding from your body. Mother Earth is gently catching them as they fall through the bed and down into the soil. Imagine that the Earth is removing these old energies for you. She is purifying you.

If you fall asleep during this process, that's great. Sleep is so healing, particularly when you're navigating big emotions. However, if you don't fall asleep, that's okay too. Whatever happens, allow yourself to use the comfort and security of your bed to give yourself full permission to feel what you're feeling.

As you allow the emotion of anger to flow freely, you may be flooded with memories of past traumatic events. If this happens, give yourself a hug. Watch these memories effortlessly fall from your body, releasing into Mother Earth.

Throughout this process, it's likely that tears may come. Don't hold back these tears. If you feel like you need to shout or moan or vocalize some other primal sounds, do it! This is not a time for logic and politeness. This is a time to release that old gunk.

After a few minutes or a few hours (give yourself permission to take as long as you need), you will emerge from the cocoon of your bed with a more calm, peaceful mind. At this point, if protective or corrective actions need to be taken in the outer world (such as creating new boundaries, leaving abusive relationships, or adopting healthier lifestyle habits), then take some time to journal about your potential next steps.

CHAPTER 3

DEEPENING THANKS: THE THIRD PRECEPT

There is no greater prayer than gratitude.

Things remain the same

until the day

we find ourselves grateful

for things as they are.

ALFRED SAVINELLI

There are innumerable angels, spirit guides, and Beings of Light whose sole purpose is to help you with your Reiki journey.

Whether we connect with archangels Michael or Raphael, commune with ancient avatars such as Rama or Krishna, or meditate with the wonderful souls from our Reiki lineage such as Usui or Takata, having a grateful recognition of these helper beings will build our spiritual confidence tremendously. Over time, by connecting with them, we build trust that we are not alone in the Universe. We know—within our very blood—that we are supported.

The act of saying Thank You is a perfection of the third precept, "Be grateful." At the beginning and end of each meditation and Reiki healing session, the best thing that we can do is to thank our guides. By thanking them, we invite them to reveal their presence to us.

In truth, we don't need to say anything other than thank you. In other words, we don't need to make any kind of request. We don't need to pray "Please cure my illness" or "Please bring me wisdom." *As these cosmic beings are not limited by time or space, they already know the contents of our innermost heart.* Therefore, all that's left for us to do is to bow in humble gratitude.

Practice Invitation

To practice the third Reiki precept, perform the following Thank You Ritual.

Bring your hands together in *gassho* (palm to palm) in front of your heart. Take a breath and say thank you, aloud or internally. You can address specific beings by name or you can be more general and simply say, for example: "Thank you, angels" or "Thank you, guides" or "Thank you, my dear ancestors."

Next, raise your gassho up to your forehead, resting the knuckles of your thumbs against your third eye chakra (between the eyebrows). Take another breath and say thank you again.

Finally, drop to your knees and bow, surrendering your forehead to Mother Earth. Take one more breath, saying thank you.

As you offer these thanks, observe how the energy flows within your body. Do you feel more peaceful? More safe? Do you hear comforting messages from your guides? Do you feel a warm presence? Do you see or sense visions? Do you feel sensations such as tingling or pulsing? Simply observe whatever is arising and feel gratitude.

CHAPTER 4

THE FOURTH PRECEPT: BEING TRUE

With passion pray.

With passion work.

With passion make love.

With passion eat and drink

and dance and play.

Why look like a dead fish

in this ocean of God?

RUMI

Many of my students have found the fourth Reiki precept—"Be true to your way and your True Self"—as the most confusing of all the precepts.

Through these sacred words, we are being invited into a seemingly paradoxical situation: to balance and find truth within two very different things.

The uncapitalized phrase "your way" is referring to the ego's dualistic desires. We are being invited to *consciously embrace* (rather than shun) these unique desires. To be true to your way means to give the small self, the personality, the point of uniqueness that is 'me/I' on this human journey a soothing, peaceful hug.

In other words, the first part of this precept is an invitation to soften. We are being asked to release any rigid, moralistic perspectives about the ego and relax into a gentler, more compassionate view.

For what is ego other than passion?

For what is ego other than the unique dance of life?

Let us never forget that it is desire that creates this entire Universe! This glorious *lila* (divine play) needs desire to exist! Therefore, let us not bemoan the ego (the uniqueness of life). Let us, in fact, celebrate!

Indeed, this is the new paradigm here on New Earth. No more hating the ego; no more condemning it.

In a sense, we could say that the ego is—for all of us—in a constant process of dying. Of dissolving. By practicing the fourth precept, then, we share with our ego a peaceful end: a kind of compassionate hospice care.

Eventually, yes, the ego will return back to Source. But, until that time, what to do?

A wise Buddhist nun, Jetsunma Tenzin Palmo, teaches that awakening is humanity's destiny. We are all on the path and we will all bloom in perfect timing. No need to rush and no need to worry about measuring up to some lofty goals. In a wonderful talk shared on Youtube, she says: "Forget enlightenment. The important thing is just to be now and here."[3] I agree with this statement wholeheartedly! Let us dare to release our mind's grip on the future, on our eagerness to arrive. Instead, let us simply observe and appreciate how we are being pulled, as if by a magical magnet, toward Source. Toward our True Home.

Of course, yes, let us continue our daily Reiki practice—but not because we 'should' do it in order to 'attain' something … but rather, let the motivation for our practice come from a deeper place, from a simple wish to experience *a full and beautiful life in the here and now.*

Indeed, for those of us who have been indoctrinated into various religions and traditions, what I'm saying right now may seem radical. I understand this. But this is a crucial point. To dare to *embrace the ego*—rather than despise it or run away from it—is a major accomplishment on the spiritual path. For eons, most of the world's religious traditions advocated a shunning of the ego. But this is not the deepest truth for many of us and, therefore, such false teachings are now disappearing from Planet Earth! In order to discover peace in our lives, what's most helpful is simply to be more honest and aware of our own unique ways of being an embodied human. Rather than wishing away the ego, we need to be *more* authentic, *more* true to the quirks of how our soul wants to manifest in this incarnation.

In this way, our Heart can sigh in relief. No more pretending, no more barreling ahead, no more grasping after overly-lofty spiritual goals. Instead, let us breathe, embrace our uniqueness on the journey, and take our time.

Ultimately, "Be true to your way and your True Self" is an invitation to embrace the you that you've resisted or denied.

---

3 "Straight Talk About #Enlightenment" talk available on the Dharma Time channel

23

In my journey, for example, it has taken me decades to openly admit that I am, at heart, a creature of solitude. I adore living alone and I do not wish to have children. For me, the most ecstatic times of life include long stretches of hermiting in my home as well as solo camping excursions out into the most remote, wild places. However, for many years, I felt ashamed of these desires and tried to hide them. I felt that others would judge me as lazy, selfish, or antisocial. Thanks to the insight of the fourth precept, however, I stopped hiding who I am. I realized that it's *vital* for my unique soul journey to take lots of alone time—and I don't need to apologize for that!

Indeed, each one of us is born with unique *samskaras*: psychological patterns, preferences, and habitual tendencies incurred from past lifetimes. Our soul carries these imprints each time we are reborn into a body. A major aim of our spiritual practice is to honor these unique samskaras and discover how the path can unfold perfectly for us.

By remembering the fourth precept, we get really honest with ourselves. What are our unique fears and weaknesses? What are our non-negotiables in this lifetime? What are we here to do? What are our unique skills and strengths?

Yes, some of us are painters; some of us are poets. Some of us are singers; some of us are filmmakers. Some are mothers and some are sons and lovers. Some are amazing doctors, while others journey through the jungles in search of orchids.

We're all perfect.

So, yes, the first part of the fourth precept urges us to find our unique passions, our unique gifts of service, and live them out to the fullest. We might make money from these passions or we might not.

Whatever our soul most needs for the learning journey is exactly what will happen.

∞

What, then, is the meaning behind the second part of the fourth precept?

What did Mikao Usui mean by the capitalized phrase "True Self"?

To stay true to our True Self means that we aim to move beyond the limited ego by practicing Reiki daily, by living more and more of our daily existence in a blessed state of nonduality, or as the Buddhists like to call it, *śūnyatā*.

Śūnyatā is the peace that automatically happens when we're alive without worrying, stressing, or analyzing.

Śūnyatā is surrender, allowing Spirit to move us.

We often imagine that peace is dependent upon external conditions (if this person would only say this, if that politician would only enact that law, if those countries would only lay down their weapons, etc.)—but, in truth, the deepest peace comes through the cessation of thought. In moments when we stop the mind chatter, this is when the clear light of awareness dawns. This is Heaven on Earth. Here we rest peacefully without a name or form. Here we simply Be, we simply Are.

So, how do we balance the first part and the second part of this precept?

All we really need to do is to remember that there is no 'higher' and no 'lower' in this Universe. No hierarchy. To practice the fourth precept is to *not* pit "your way" (ego) against "True Self" (Divinity). For truly there is no battle here! What we are doing is simply cultivating

Peace! Whenever we honor our unique personality/ego, we are one step closer to permanently abiding as our True Self. This is a paradox, but it is true.

As we lovingly witness the dying process of the ego (a totally natural occurrence), we breathe with confidence that all is indeed well, that all is indeed how it's meant to be.

Ultimately, to most deeply engage with the fourth precept is to heal our fears of 'doing it wrong.' There is nothing wrong with consciously embracing the ego during its dying days!! We can observe it and bow to it, saying: *Thank you, dear ego. Thank you, dear identity. Thank you; you've served me well.*

This precept also has the benefit of helping us to become more tolerant toward our fellow human beings. As time passes, we will naturally embody a state of Being where we no longer feel the need to judge others for doing their thing. We will no longer need to judge others for what is uniquely their path to live out, on their own karmic journey. This is how world peace is made.

Practice Invitation

Observe your reactions to others during the next few days. How often are you judging your friends and family? Do you judge your coworkers? How about strangers on the street?

I notice that when I'm feeling stressed out, for example, I'll survey people's carts at the supermarket and silently judge them for making what I perceive to be unhealthy choices. (Eeek!)

Are there certain behaviors that get on your nerves? Are there any particular choices that trigger frustration, anger, or self-righteousness in you?

The next time you notice yourself judging someone (you'll probably be feeling the emotions of irritation or annoyance, which are less dramatic forms of anger), recite the fourth precept a few times. Look inward to your Heart and remind yourself that everyone is doing the very best that they can.

Finally, please remember this: The practice of releasing judgment does *not* mean that you turn off your brain and simply allow anything. Discernment is good. It's wise and healthy to analyze whether someone's values align with yours. If a person or group are acting in ways that seem unethical or simply non-resonant with how you want to live, then there is absolutely nothing wrong with peacefully stepping away. You can always love at a distance.

CHAPTER 5

LET YOURSELF OFF THE HOOK: THE FIFTH PRECEPT

Let yourself off the hook. Your heart may not always feel warm and loving—and that's okay.

Let yourself off the hook. Maybe you don't feel happy today—and that's okay.

Sometimes there are storm clouds in the skies of life.

Let yourself off the hook. Sometimes you might feel bored, irritated, depressed, lonely. All of this is okay.

Let yourself off the hook.

Accept yourself for exactly how you are *right now*.

Allow yourself to feel the relief of this.

∞

My dear friend, let yourself off the biggest (and most subtle) hook of all, which is the hook of 'trying to be a good person.' Completely drop this notion!

Paradoxically, when we stop trying so darn hard to be good—this is when we can perceive our natural goodness.

Goodness is not something we need to strive toward: goodness is our True Nature.

So often, we Reiki healers strive toward the impossible goal of always being happy, of always being full of radiant love, of always trying to 'do the right thing.' But these formulaic and rigid expectations we have of ourselves—while certainly sprouting from noble intentions—often, unfortunately, end up stalling our growth in the long run.

∞

The fifth Reiki precept—"Be compassionate to yourself and others"—might seem so obvious. Why would this need explanation? There are, however, hidden meanings within the precept.

At first glance, one might think that this precept is an injunction to meticulously monitor our behavior so that we always act with sweetness and kindness. However, to *truly* embody this precept is not necessarily about taking action in the exterior world. Rather, it's an invitation to accept ourselves *just as we are.* (This is a radical transformation, leading to accepting others just as they are.)

Through our practice of Reiki, we learn that even while traversing highly-charged emotional landscapes, we can always find some measure of peace. Even if it's only a tiny ray of sunshine within a sky of stormy thunderclouds… that Light is always present; that Light is always there.

The heart may be breaking into a million billion pieces, and yet we can still feel—simultaneously—a restful state of peace within.

Of course, we must work diligently to increase this wise perception. Embodying this way of Being truly requires a lot of unhooking! We must unhook from all the myriad social expectations, pressures, and cultural norms that tell us that to be peaceful is boring or strange. We must unhook from the tendency to put on a fake, cheerful smile. We must unhook from fears about what other people will think about our spiritual practices. And, eventually, we must learn to unhook from our deep-rooted fears about illness, old age, and death. This is, ultimately, what the practice of Reiki is all about. We relax into peaceful states of Being that are characterized by nonjudgment, equanimity, and an open-hearted trust in the Universe.

In this particular incarnation, I've often tried to showcase myself to others (and even myself!) as perpetually joyful, happy, and bursting with light. I've been fake sometimes. I've agreed to service obligations that were not aligned with my way. I've exhausted myself, gotten burnt out, and created a lot of resentment toward myself and others. This sort of exhausted striving did not honor the authentic reality of Creation.

Whether happy or hopeful, judging or jubilant, kind or comical, tired or energetic, worried or wondering, I am Anya Light and I AM OKAY.

Of course, it's wonderful to feel happy and it's amazing to feel bliss… however, let's not get lost. Our highest aim on the spiritual path is Peace. Only Peace. This is the only sustainable way. If happiness or bliss or delight or enjoyment spontaneously arise, that's great—but let us not chase these transitory states.

The more that we chase, the more frustrated we tend to become.

During difficult times, let us relax and feed ourselves the food of Love. Let us whisper to our inner heart: "It's okay to feel this way, dear one. Sometimes life is hard. Thank you for being brave enough to slow down and feel it all."

Let yourself off the hook.

Allow yourself to sink into Peace.

And observe the reactions and fears of the mind: *What if people think I'm too weird? What if I lose friends because people think I'm boring? What if peace becomes my permanent state, and I never again get to feel ecstasy or excitement or adventure? What if I never laugh again? What if I never joke or play with other humans in radiant joy? What if I never feel passionate romance again? What if I become lazy or lose interest in the world?*

As you can see, diving deep into the fifth precept is a profound undertaking! Remember that we can gently embrace such questions without needing to immediately find all the answers. In time, answers will come. Everything unfolds in perfect timing.

Being compassionate *always arrives naturally and spontaneously by choosing to embody Peace as our highest calling.* For what is True Compassion other than being the still, quiet, empty vessel for the Reiki energy to flow through? Therefore, when our minds are busy and the world seems to be on fire all around us, the best course of action is to simply settle down and center ourselves with the breath. Allow any fears and emotions to arise without judgment.

As we practice Peace as our highest calling, as we accept and allow all emotions to flow through us, we give permission to other souls to embrace the raw, messy nature of the human experience.

On New Earth, we're updating the idea of being human. For eons, it was assumed that to be human—to have a human heart—is something lower, something ugly, something to be quickly 'transcended' and forgotten about. In reality, though, to be a human being is a great gift.

It is the ability to breathe through the storm clouds.

It is the ability to laugh, even when all hope is gone.

Practice Invitation

Take an inventory of your relationships and social situations.

Are there certain settings where you feel obligated to always be smiling or cheerful? Do you feel like, in these places, you always need to be 'on'?

Are there certain people in your life who expect you to be a certain way?

Do you find yourself desperately trying to prove (to yourself or others) that you're a 'nice person' or a 'good person'?

Do you sometimes take on too many social commitments or service obligations? Do you give yourself enough quiet/alone time?

Do you sometimes feel like you're pretending or faking?

Do you sometimes feel like you're trying to mold yourself into who others expect you to be?

For the next month, I invite you to embrace Peace (neutrality/calm/ inner stillness) as your highest priority on the spiritual path. Let yourself off the hook. You no longer need to chase feelings of happiness or excitement or passion. You don't even have to smile!! Simply embrace the Peace that is your True Nature. Simply BE as you ARE.

CHAPTER 6

CLEAN YOUR
HOUSE FIRST

In this day and age of instant internet communication, apps for everything, and same-day Amazon delivery, it can sometimes feel difficult to pace ourselves. This is especially true when we're excited about something.

On the Reiki path, the practice of hands-on healing requires patience. Even though the ego may want to be an All-Star Healer right now, even though the ego might desperately want to lay hands on the whole world today... what's really needed, most of all, is patience.

What we need to do, as healers, is take the long view.

In most Reiki courses in the West, it's common for beginning students to learn how to do hands-on healing for other people. (This is common practice even amongst teachers whom I greatly admire.) However, I strongly believe that such a fast dive into the practice of hands-on healing is often unproductive and even potentially harmful. As I always say to my students: *Clean your house before throwing a party.*

In other words, in the beginning stages of your Reiki journey, spend a few months (at least) completely devoted to healing yourself. Touch your own inner peace before seeking to touch others.

Healer, heal thyself.

In my curriculum, for example, I require *Shoden* (Level One) graduates to wait at least two months before applying to my *Okuden* (Level Two) class. This gives folks enough time to clear out the hidden cobwebs before proceeding to invite others into their home.

Offering Reiki healing sessions to other beings is a sacred, highly intimate act—one not to be underestimated in its magnitude. Thus, it is good to take our time to prepare ourselves before we work so closely with others. For if we cannot hold space for another in a balanced, pure way, then the Universe will mirror our ignorance back to us. For example, if we rush headlong into healing others, we may be magnetically drawn to those who do not respect our boundaries or to those who seek more time than we can reasonably give. We may even encounter those who wish to slander us or energetically attack us by using black magic. We could also be unprepared for the tragic stories that we are bound to hear when others come to us seeking relief. (All of these scenarios happened to me in the beginning of my Reiki journey.) If we still have gaping wounds left within our Souls, then we can be sure that other people will mirror those wounds back to us. This can be a very unpleasant and triggering way to learn.

Fortunately, there's an easier way. If we take the necessary time to gently clean our own house first, then we will evolve at a rate that is not so overwhelming.

The slow path is the path to Peace.

Just as we are careful about the people with whom we share a bed, so too is it wise to be cautious about immersing ourselves into other people's energy fields. Yes, Reiki is amazing, and of course we long to share it... and, *also*, taking on the role of a public healer is a *big, big* responsibility.

I share this advice from personal experience. I learned the hard way. When I consider the breakneck pace that characterized the early part of my journey, I see how stressful it was. At times I felt completely overwhelmed, as if I was standing on sinking sand. I had some intense and, admittedly, traumatizing encounters with students which exposed my karma in ways that rocked me to the core. Looking back, I can see that it would have been preferable to have built more of a solid inner foundation before externalizing my journey with others.

Nevertheless, I hold deep gratitude in my heart, because what happened to me was meant to happen. I learned the hard way so that I could teach my students a better way.

Practice Invitation #1

If you're a first-degree Reiki practitioner and are already facilitating hands-on healing sessions for other human beings, I strongly urge you to pause. Turn that energy back to yourself and devote a few months to your own self-healing. Practice the precepts daily. Meditate daily.

If you are a second-degree or Master-level practitioner, notice the times in your life when you're being called to pause and simply bask in the glory of your own two hands.

Indeed, do not hesitate to withdraw from the outer world, as needed, in order to deepen your practice. This may come in times of grief or in times of intense transition. Perhaps you may need to withdraw from the world when you feel overwhelmed with responsibilities or you feel energetically burnt out.

Whenever you feel this way, there's many options. You could go camping, rent a quiet cabin in the woods, book a meditation retreat, or simply refrain from scheduling Reiki sessions for a few weeks. Take some time for self-care. Take some time to feel into the dark corners that are asking for the light of your own self-love. Be daring enough to take rest.

If you're feeling impatient to share hands-on healings with others, for whatever reason, draw the *Choku Rei* symbol on your feet and pray for the courage to walk slowly, trusting in the Divine timing of the Universe. (If you're unfamiliar with this symbol, that's okay. Simply pray the prayer and imagine your feet moving slowly through this world with grace.)

How will you know when you're ready to return from your retreat? A sign that you're ready is that you feel a sense of inner peace and quietude. Check within: If you still feel emotionally perturbed or your mind is spinning, then you're probably not ready to resume your work with others. If you sense, however, a deep sense of tranquility, then you are ready to get out there and share again! Enjoy!!

Practice Invitation #2

In the West, we want things right now—RIGHT RIGHT RIGHT NOW!!! Hence, a sort of "fast food Reiki" has emerged: the kind of Reiki where you can get certified in ten minutes online or become a 'master' in a single weekend. How silly.

While the ego may thrive on instant gratification, the Soul craves something more.

Reflect back upon your Reiki training. Consider that some teachers offer, for example, a Master's course that takes a year or more to complete. Or that many teachers offer in-depth, Level One and Two training that span a few weeks or even a few months.

Ask yourself: Are you craving additional training? Do you feel called to repeat a level with a different teacher? Take some time to journal about your past learning experiences and ask if your Heart is wanting more.

CHAPTER 7

OUR INHERENT FREEDOM

Compassion is not a relationship
between the healer and the wounded.
It's a relationship between equals.

PEMA CHÖDRÖN

The people with whom we share healing may not understand what
we do. They may have difficulty understanding that the Light simply
travels *through* us. They may not understand that we ourselves do
not create that Light, do not author that Light.

The truth is: There is nothing that we healers 'do' at all! What happens during a Reiki healing is actually a *lack* of doing. A surrendering. What happens is that we Stop. We merge into the Oneness.

Through the release of ego, the Light shines bright.

Thus, as we joyously share Reiki healing with our fellow human being
on Earth, let us never accept praise on behalf of the small self. Let us

never accept any pedestal. Instead, let our lives be colored by a gentle humility. Let us give all the credit to the God who works through us.

We Reiki practitioners are channels. Or, as our Native American friends say: the healer is a "hollow bone." When we emanate the vibrations of healing touch, uplifting word, or a loving glance, we remind people of the truth of their Divinity.

One of the most common pitfalls you may encounter on the Reiki path is to misunderstand your role. Instead of being an empty vessel, the ego may try to take control. You may start to feel responsible for other people's journeys. You may get embroiled into emotional attachments. Your relationships might feel messy, confusing, or codependent. You might sometimes feel like a worried, overbearing parent. Or, even worse, you may begin to feel that people owe you something.

As Reiki practitioners, we are not 'special.' We are not 'chosen.' In reality, what we are is nothing! No one! In our truest, deepest Being, the 'me' vanishes and God takes over. This is how true healing happens. This is how Peace on Earth is created.

Practice Invitation

To cultivate healthy relationships—free from negative karma and entanglements, please repeat the following mantra:

"You are free. You are free. How may I serve you?"

This powerful, yet simple mantra reminds you that you're here on Planet Earth to serve a specific function: to assist in the global awakening process. You do this by becoming as clear of a channel as possible. In other words, it's *not* your job to take personal credit for this work. Nobody owes you anything.

The mechanism of control that was so prevalent on old earth is dying. You are here to birth new ways of Being. When you repeat the mantra "You are free. You are free. How may I serve you?"...say these words from the depths of your Soul. Imagine that your Soul is speaking directly to their Soul. Trust that they are receiving the message.

By chanting this mantra, you detach from the thoughts, feelings, sensations, and perceptions that create negative karmic loops. In this way, your work (whether paid or not) becomes pure *seva* (sacred service).

Also, be prepared that when you say this mantra, many of your relations will undergo a profound shift.

Sometimes, the answer to the question "how may I serve" will be to offer more Reiki sessions to the person—but in a different way. You may need to change your approach: for example, maybe the exchange of money needs to drop away, or perhaps you will stop using tactile touch. Or, perhaps the location at which sessions are offered will need to change.

Or, it may happen that, through the clarity of this mantra, you realize that it's time to radically alter the form of the relationship itself. Perhaps the partner with whom you shared Reiki is no longer aligned to be your partner—so you let them go with unconditional love in your heart. Or, perhaps your student has graduated from your teachings, so you encourage them to leave the nest and study with a different teacher. Or, perhaps you are no longer aligned to be in a close friendship with someone and so you request new boundaries within the context of a gentle, compassionate conversation.

By practicing this important mantra, you master the art of peaceful relationships. You model new ways to love and be loved in return.

CHAPTER 8

PEACE DAYS

Every day we are faced with a million decisions. Should we eat this or eat that? Should we buy this or buy that? Talk to this person or walk away? Continue this relationship or not?

In this busy world of so many options, our minds are on overdrive. We are constantly yearning for the happy times of the past or worried about all the crazy things that might happen in the future. In these anxious mental states, our crown chakra (the powerful energetic portal located at the top of the head) remains mostly closed.

But then... we remember Reiki—and we are suddenly not so worried. We open ourselves up to the peaceful flow of energy that's always been there. Our minds get quiet. Our bodies uncoil. We remember that Divinity is guiding every step.

In the following practice, *Peace Days*, I share a simple way that we can open up to experience the Reiki energy more deeply. The Universe gifted me the vision of this practice during a chapter in my life when I was extremely ill and depressed. As I was unable to leave my bed, what else could I do but practice? While I sincerely hope that you never have to deal with such an incredibly difficult health ordeal, I do hope that you will *consciously choose* to practice *Peace Days* in order to fast-track your evolution. Don't wait for illness or tragedy to strike. Embrace the practice now and reap the blessings.

Practice Invitation

In *Shoden* (Level One) training, you were taught to use your hands to initiate healing. However, as your relationship with the Reiki energy deepens, you realize that hands are merely a starting point.

The next time you rise in the morning and feel any sort of discomfort (physical illness, fatigue, worry, anger, etc.), dedicate your entire day to the practice of Reiki. Call this your *Peace Day*.

On this beautiful, most precious day, you will peacefully complete your daily tasks while constantly absorbing the healing Reiki energy.

There are two methods for practice on *Peace Day*. First, as you move throughout your day, pay attention to your breath. Visualize that you are pulling the Reiki energy down into your crown with each inhale. On each exhale, circulate the energy throughout your whole body. As your day progresses, there will (of course) be moments, minutes, or even possibly hours when you'll forget this intention. Know that's okay! Such forgetting is completely normal. Simply bring your awareness back to breathing into the crown, again and again and again.

The second method for practice during your *Peace Day* is to imagine that your entire body is a sponge. The Reiki energy—effortlessly and joyously—is penetrating your sponge-body and filling all parts of you.

You can intuitively alternate between these two methods throughout the day. You may discover, at a certain point, that one of these ways resonates a bit more with you, and so you'll naturally find yourself doing that particular one more. If so, that's great! Whatever happens, the key is to relax and enjoy.

As both of these practices are fairly simple, you can do them while accomplishing other tasks, such as cooking, cleaning, walking, talking, paying bills, gardening, looking after children, and so on. One of the wonderful outcomes of this practice is that you will become less and less dependent upon hand positions and, consequently, discover how the *entire human vessel* is naturally prepared to receive the Reiki healing energy—anywhere, anytime.

You'll notice too how your human relationships soften and become more peaceful and loving. You'll notice a greater sense of harmony, a greater sense of flow and Oneness in all your interactions. The higher your vibration goes, the more you meet others on the same plane.

By practicing these nourishing *Peace Days*, you're committing to a life of Reiki. You're becoming a master in the truest sense.

I recommend practicing *Peace Days* whenever your schedule feels extra busy. They are also helpful whenever you're facing challenges, changes, or upgrades in your human relationships. Dedicating whole days to your Reiki practice will allow you to appreciate how healing is much, much more than simply closing your eyes and laying hands upon yourself. When you surrender your days to the peaceful flow of Reiki as a constant awareness, you'll tune into the deepest wisdom within the Universe. You'll unlock wisdom that was, heretofore, inaccessible to you. You will vibrate differently.

As you enjoy your *Peace Days*, you'll feel and understand the deepest Truth about our practice: Reiki is not something that we 'channel' into us...Reiki *is* us. We *are* Reiki.

CHAPTER 9

GRATITUDE FOR THE BODY

Instead of trying to move quickly forward,
we need to slowly go through
whatever needs to be fixed on our journey.
There is no rush to go anywhere but here.
In fact, the greater our hurry to arrive
where we think we want to be spiritually,
the longer it will take,
since our conceptions will still be
unrealistic and implausible.
Actual spirituality means there is no escape
and no need for escape.
And it also means utter freedom through limitation
and every sort of difficulty.

SWAMI PADMANABHA

An important part of the Reiki healing process is to make peace with the human body. When we place our loving hands upon ourselves and others, what we are essentially doing is integrating the wisdom of the body with the wisdom of Soul. We are learning that these two things are, in fact, One.

However, we may become confused when we read ancient scriptures that teach about the illusions of this material world or that the body is 'lower' or 'bad.'

These teachings, on one level, are not wrong. Our body can indeed be a source of misery, and it is true that our truest identity is not the material body. What we Are is truly vast...

What we Are—at the deepest level—is immortal, untouchable, pristine, and impenetrable from the ravages of time.

What we Are is a piece of God!

However, understanding this Truth on an intellectual level does *not* negate the reality of our lives here and now. The beauty of the Reiki path is that it allows us to balance our True Self (our God Self) with our individual self (our blessed ego). (Please see Chapter Four for more of these teachings.) In other words, the Reiki path is about balancing Ultimate Knowledge of ourselves as God with the very real reality of our present situation as a mortal human being!!

If we look carefully, these two things are *not* in contradiction. On the one hand, yes, what we truly Are is Soul/Spirit/Ātman/Formlessness/Emptiness/God (whatever label you want to call it). By keeping this in mind, we can work towards our ultimate goal: To fully know ourselves beyond the material human body and to transcend all fears of death.

However, on the other hand, *right now* we appear to be human beings! And that's very real too. We are playing the role of a sacred individual: a body and personality that moves through space and time, a body and being that expresses needs and preferences. Right now, we have eyes that see and lungs that breathe. Yes! Great!

So, we are both human and Divine. Okay. But...how do we actually *live* these two simultaneous, seemingly contradictory truths? How do we integrate *both* ways of seeing? How do we solve this paradox?

∞

During this time of collective global awakening, what is needed most right now are many doses of gentle self-love.

We Reiki practitioners have been called back to Planet Earth to try an entirely new paradigm: to demonstrate compassion for the individual self. To not merely cope with the ego, but to actually *Love* the ego.

Wow, how remarkable!!!

This is such an important chapter for human beings on the spiritual path. We are waking up to a new level of knowledge: that we cannot transcend what we do not—first—Love.

Thus, it is good to approach our Reiki practice in such a way that will help us to remember that our ultimate identity is not the body, while *also* embracing the current reality of our situation in human form.

In other words, before we are fully stabilized in our Buddha Nature beyond the body (the highest level of wisdom, the level of the saints and sages), we must *first* go through a grounded period of *fully embracing the body as a manifestation of the Divine.*

This is hard work—but we *can* do it!! The key is to move slowly. To be patient with ourselves.

Imagine trying to teach calculus to a first-grader. Obviously, that would be impossible! By the same means, the goal of fully transcending the body is usually chased far too early on the spiritual path. Such impatient strivings often devolve into neglecting, mistreating, or even outright abuse of the body. This is what we did in so many past lifetimes, and we are now ready to evolve.

Instead of transcendence being the only goal, dear friend, let us instead slow down and cultivate a healthy passage of gratitude. Let us dive into a period when we rejoice in the Divine Miracle that is our physical form on Earth. Let us gradually ease into the awakening process by first allowing ourselves the breathing room to consciously and joyously experience our humanity.

As we do this, it's important to remember that we live in a truly wonderful age. Let's be grateful! We have the opportunity to integrate the timeless, mystical teachings of the East (meditation, reincarnation, karma, etc.) into the beautiful and grounded psychological teachings of the West (emotional patterns, trauma, conscious relating). Yes, this is a truly exciting time to be alive! Both of these ways of knowing are necessary for our evolution.

Yes, right now we are experiencing a powerful leap as a collective. Spiritual seekers everywhere are learning to treat their body as a temple, as a gorgeous vessel that flows the Light of God. Rather than constantly thinking about the ultimate unreality of the body or bemoaning the dis-eases and limitations of the body, what's happening right now is a *conscious dwelling within the body with immense Gratitude.*

Practice Invitation

For the next four days, I invite you to begin your day with a prayer of gratitude. Feel thanks that you are alive in human form.

As you pray this prayer, speak to your body as you would a dear friend. Here's some examples of some words you might use:

Thank you, dear hands, for holding this book.

Thank you, dear legs, for carrying me to school today.

I am grateful to you, sweet stomach, for digesting this food.

As you pray these prayers, lovingly touch the corresponding parts of your body with your enlightened Reiki Hands. Feel the energy flow.

After you've completed four days of this practice, assess how you feel. If your intuition guides you, you may extend this practice to four weeks. (The number four is symbolic of building strong foundations and habits.) If you feel called, keep notes about your unfolding journey and share your experience with others.

CHAPTER 10

NOURISHING THE BODY

O human, see then the human being rightly:
the human being has heaven and earth
and the whole of creation in itself,
and yet is a complete form,
and in it everything is already present,
though hidden.

HILDEGARD OF BINGEN

In bygone eras and other lifetimes, we wished to escape our bodies. We hated and denigrated them. Catholics whipped themselves with nails. Hindus ate one grain of rice per day. Jews had elaborate rituals for purifying their 'uncleanliness.' Indeed, in the collective story of humankind, religion and the body have been sworn enemies.

Thankfully, things are changing now! The Reiki community, as well as spiritual circles across the globe, are waking up to a new reality: The body can be a friend!

We humans are learning that heaping love and blessings upon the body is *not* vanity (as older eras believed). Rather, loving the body is an expedient way to upgrade our consciousness. By loving the body, we discover that God is not separate from the body. God is ALL! God is EVERYTHING: the sky, the grass, the rain, the rocks, the human body, EVERYTHING!

My dear friend, the body is *alive*! The body is a beating heart of Divinity! Every cell worships the name of God. Every bone and tissue cry out the Truth that we are One.

In this world with so much distraction, it takes actual courage to nourish the body. It is no small act! To do it may feel awkward or even terrifying. (The level of difficulty depends upon how much trauma we have yet to resolve.) Indeed, we might notice that as we whisper nourishing words to our bodies or engage in self-love practices, that a reaction of irritation or perhaps even disgust may arise. If this happens, know that's perfectly okay. We can simply witness each feeling and each thought with Love. We can be patient.

There's so many ways to nourish our bodies. We can purchase, prepare, or even grow our own food (rather than grabbing the fast, easy option). More mindfulness around our food journey simultaneously nourishes the body as well as nourishes Mother Earth, the female body from which we came. We can also bring more movement into our daily lives, such as yoga, dance, tai chi, swimming, or walking. More movement means that we most effectively circulate the Reiki energy within us, opening our channels to greater insight and peace.

As we explore this nourishing healing process, let us remember—most importantly!—to be patient with ourselves. If we have suffered from intense trauma or debilitating illness in the past, such a conscious return to the body may at times feel quite challenging. It may bring up all sorts of hidden emotions and fears. Our minds may sometimes race with doubt…

Am I being self-indulgent by focusing so much on myself?

Am I wrong to pursue my own relief and happiness?

Shouldn't I be spending more time in the service of others?

These sorts of questions are a hangover from earlier eras, when we were taught that it's selfish to love ourselves. And while it's perfectly valid to go through a period of doubt, ultimately, with time and patience, we realize that disconnection from the body is a collective core wound that is desperately calling out for healing.

Ultimately, the more we do to nourish our bodies with Love, the more we give permission to others to do the same.

What I heal in me is what you heal in you.

The individual heals so that the collective can heal.

We are all on this healing journey together.

In truth, we are all One Body.

Practice Invitation

The Reiki self-healing session is a unifying experience. It is a miraculous moment when the hands of your body give to your own body. It is a simultaneous giving and receiving, a simultaneous teaching and learning. It's the collapse of duality.

In this practice, I invite you to nourish the parts of you that have felt the most disconnected. I invite you to reclaim the parts that have been relegated to the shadows.

Is there a part of your body that you don't like? Many people in the West, for example, don't like their feet. (They think their feet are deformed, smelly, etc.) Or many women hate their hips and breasts. (Because these shapes fail to live up to mass media standards.) For many men, they feel embarrassed that their arms do not have enough muscle.

Is there an area of your body that evokes negative emotion or that you judge as ugly or weak? Perhaps there is an area that you've considered to be a 'problem area': a part that has been plagued by illness.

This evening, before bed, give that area of your body a gentle massage. If possible, use organic oils or aromatherapy. Infuse each stroke with the nourishing Light of Reiki.

Keep your eyes open during the massage, sending the Reiki healing energy through your gaze. (If the body part you're healing is on your face or located in an area that is difficult to see, you can use a mirror.)

As you nourish your body with both sacred touch and gaze, feel the peace of Wholeness, of all the parts coming together as One.

Feel how, by nourishing your sacred vessel, a feeling of completion enters your Heart.

CHAPTER 11

HEALING ADDICTIONS WITH LOVE

Before we find Reiki, we try all sorts of things. We may get hooked to screens. We may use substances or spend too much money. We may bounce from lover to lover. Or, we may obsessively travel, endlessly craving new friends and new experiences.

Addiction is a frantic searching on the outside. It's an attempt to use the outside world as a way to fix the inside.

Fortunately, addiction cannot last very long in the nurturing rays of Reiki. As we channel this Infinite Healing Energy, we discover that peace is not obtained by any external person, place, or thing. Rather, peace is obtained within.

On the Reiki path, the energy of addiction gets transmuted. It gets re-directed towards our Life Purpose. More and more, as we practice the Reiki meditations, precepts, and self-healing sessions, we have visions of the more-aligned life we wish to lead. We feel greater clarity. It becomes easier to step away from what no longer serves us.

For example, perhaps we've used alcohol as a way to relax during social situations. Yet, since we've been attuned to Reiki, we feel hangovers ever-more intensely! Why would we continue drinking? It just doesn't make sense.

Or perhaps we've gotten accustomed to spending our weekends with wild, chaotic people. They've brought a certain excitement, a certain thrill to our lives. However, since entering the world of Reiki, we now find our Hearts yearning for more peaceful, quiet, Light-filled companions. So, when our old pals call us up on the phone, it's quite easy to decline their invitations.

Or, maybe for years we've habitually turned to caffeine to bring energy and inspiration to an otherwise boring job… but now, having been trained in Reiki, we're having dreams of building a truly meaningful vocation, one that would bring vitality and joy into our lives.

It's amazing! Reiki ushers in the new, while also gently helping us to release the old.

∞

In my early and mid-twenties, before I found Reiki, I was severely addicted to alcohol, cigarettes (over 2 packs a day), sugar, and fast food. However, once I got onto the Reiki path, my obsession with these substances began to fade. Eventually, the appeal of these things dissolved altogether. It wasn't that I necessarily 'tried' to stop them— rather, it was simply that I was able to see these substances for what they truly were.

Addiction is not healed through willpower.

Let me repeat that: Addiction is not healed through willpower.

Rather, addiction is healed through the light of Love. By adopting the Love-filled practices of Reiki, we automatically have less room for all the old ways.

As it turns out, my problem was not the sugar. My problem was that I didn't know how to love myself.

My problem was not the alcohol. My problem was that, deep down, I was lonely. I didn't know how to properly connect with others. Ultimately, using alcohol was my unskilled attempt at numbing the emotions of self-doubt and shame.

And, of course, it wasn't that fast food was the problem! The problem was that I hadn't yet learned how to cook nourishing meals for myself.

Through the blessed path of Reiki, we are able to unravel our deepest, most frightening conditioning. As children, it was too often that love and affection were doled out as a reward for 'correct' behavior. Thus, we got the impression that we had to be a 'good boy' or a 'good girl' in order to deserve love. How deeply traumatizing that was! Thus, as innocent children, we became experts at delivering exactly what the adults expected of us. We got very good at not only following their rules but also memorizing their judgments. Over time, we internalized their beliefs. Over time, in essence, *we became our parents.* Over time, in essence, *we became our teachers.* Over time, in essence, we *became our broken society.* We took on their conditioning and their trauma. We took on their lineage of pain. We forgot that God could fill us. We forgot our True Divine Nature.

In this horrible space of sadness, we then turned to addictions to try to fill the void.

On the supremely gentle path of Reiki, we discover self-compassion. Healing is not about being super strict with ourselves. It's not about forcing new behaviors or shaming ourselves when things don't go the way we hope. No. Those kinds of Old Earth Ways don't work anymore—and, in truth, they never worked!! Think of the person who heroically refuses the 'evils' of chocolate for Lent and then gorges themselves on Easter. Or think of the person who quits alcohol but then takes up smoking instead. When we try to use raw willpower, we are usually going to have an energetic backlash.

Therefore, the way forward is compassion.

By allowing ourselves the freedom to simply BE as we are, by learning to love ourselves unconditionally, by practicing Reiki as much as we can, then the misguided old habits will naturally fall away in time.

Here's an analogy. Imagine that you own an old convertible car. This car is beautiful and you've loved it for many years. You have had so many fond memories with it. However, it's constantly breaking down and constantly leaving you stranded on the side of the road. No fun! As time passes, due to the stress of the breakdowns, your love for the car begins to wane and you begin fantasizing about getting a new one. At the same time, however, you also don't know how to move forward. Your bank account is still too low, so you feel stuck.

One day, a friend says to you, "My dearest friend, I love you so much. I have a brand-new vehicle that I'd love to give to you. It's a really plain-looking van, though. Nothing fancy or beautiful like your convertible. Would you like it?" Of course, your friend's proposal is a no-brainer! Of course you would say yes! You are so grateful!

Every day, thereafter, you drive your new van with ease and joy. Due to sentimental reasons, you might keep your old convertible parked in the garage for a few months, and maybe even drive it a few more times, but eventually—after it breaks down for the umpteenth time—you retire that old car to the junkyard. Its day is simply done.

Our addictions are just like that. Would we continue to drive that old car (partake of the addiction) if a newer one (a better habit) came into our lives? Would we choose to get stranded on the side of the road if, instead, we had an option for a more peaceful, harmonious experience? Of course not. By the same token, we won't continue participating in an addiction if we see that there is a newer, better way to live.

Reiki shows us that better way to live.

Ultimately, all of our addictions have an expiration date. Reiki simply does not allow the cloud of ignorance to continue for very long. As we continue walking the path of Reiki, we will be guided every step of the way. We will be gifted so many miracles, so many fresh winds of possibility. Our minds will become clear. No more forcing; no more willpower needed!

If we look closely, we will see that we are *not* actually craving the ups and downs of the addiction. We are not craving the roller coaster of hangovers and poor health and shattered relationships that come along with addictive behavior. No. What we are *truly* craving is Peace.

Indeed, what we truly want most is a freely-accessible, internally-generated Peace.

My friend, the paradoxical truth is this: To find lasting healing, stop the fight! Stop the heroic efforts of willpower. Don't fight the alcohol, don't fight the drugs, don't fight the sugar. Stop fighting it all. Stop trying to fix. Instead, give yourself permission to relax and accept what's happening without judgment. It's totally okay to park that old convertible if we feel we're not quite ready to fully let it go. However, the more we practice Reiki, the new van will effortlessly become the choice we make. Eventually, we won't even *want* the convertible anymore.

As we build our reservoir of self-love, as we reunite with God through the myriad practices of Reiki, we find real and deep changes in our lives. And yes, this process takes time. Be patient with yourself! If old habits linger for a while, that's okay. Simply recollect, time and time again, a preferred vision of your future. Remember the person you wish to become: a Great Bright Light, shining for all the world to see.

Practice Invitation #1

The next time you fantasize about partaking in some old addictive behavior, simply remember that Reiki self-healing makes you feel really, really good. Allow yourself the option of partaking in that addictive behavior tomorrow, if you so choose. But in the meantime, today is the day for giving yourself Reiki healing.

Just for today, love yourself through Reiki.

Practice Invitation #2

If you're giving yourself lots of Reiki healing and you still feel drawn to partake in an old, addictive behavior, give yourself permission to do so—but do it as mindfully as possible. Do it as consciously as possible. Partake in that old, outdated behavior with yourself as a witness. Do not harshly judge yourself. Simply give yourself permission to do it and then love yourself *throughout the process.*

The key is to become aware of your emotions. If you're wanting to partake of an old behavior that feels outdated to you, ask yourself: Am I feeling sadness right now? Boredom? Anxiety? Restlessness? Anger? Notice your emotions before, during, and after you partake. And notice your thoughts? Are you falling prey to an old storyline that is driving your behavior? For example, are you trying to quell some deep, internal fears through partaking?

Also, notice if there is an inner voice that entices, justifies, blames, or shames you throughout this process. If you do notice such a voice, replace those dark words with light-filled words. With one hand on your heart, tell yourself: "I love you. I'm always going to be here for you no matter what. I love you exactly the way you are."

After you partake of that old behavior, take note of any withdrawal symptoms or after-effects. Simply note them as a scientist would (in a neutral, factual way), without getting angry or judgmental against yourself. Simply note what happens after you partake. Do you feel tired? Drained? Depressed? Unmotivated? Cloudy thinking? Nightmares? Physical tremors? Don't try to numb or cover up these after-effects. Rather, allow yourself to *feel these sensations fully*.

This is the process of rewiring your brain into new patterns. Over time, your brain will simply know, without a shadow of a doubt, that Reiki (the new behavior in your life that has no negative side effects) is much more preferable to that old addiction. Over time, you will realize your *true preference* over and over, as you effortlessly make the most uplifted choices. Addictions will naturally drift out of your life.

Practice Invitation #3

If you're feeling called to old ways, simply remind yourself of the purpose of why you're here. You're here on Planet Earth to be a Light. You are here to serve.

Reflect on all the ways that the old behavior saps your energy.

Take a few minutes and journal about all the opportunities for *seva* (sacred service) that are available to you this week and write an answer to the question: "Will my partaking of this old activity reduce my energy levels and impede my ability to serve?"

CHAPTER 12

I AM

The question 'Who am I?'

is not really meant to get an answer.

The question 'Who am I?'

is meant to dissolve the questioner.

SRI RAMANA MAHARSHI

The truth is this: Reiki practice is actually a state of non-doing. Ultimately, it's rest.

Reiki is the Peace of Being.

By surrendering to the practice of Reiki, we allow our human identity to fall away. What dissolves are all the boxes, concepts, labels, worries, and to-do lists that have caged us for eons. We enter the Light of Love.

When we fully allow this process of dissolving, we are tracing our steps back. We're journeying back to that placeless place, that timeless time: back to the ever-present I AM.

I AM is never hampered by fear or judgment. There is no separation in I AM. It is only Unity, only Oneness.

Ironically, the individual person can never know the presence of I AM. It is only when we release the perception that we are an individual (release the ego) that our truest nature can be experienced.

It is by returning to the blessed I AM that we discover the depths of peace.

Reiki is I AM and I AM is Reiki!! When we allow our hands to naturally move to the perfect place (without analysis or thought)...when we exhale with full Trust that we are perfect just as we are (without shame or self-doubt)...when we surrender the mind's worry and anger, we return to I AM. We return to Source.

Practice Invitation

Find a comfortable seated position. Close your eyes. Notice the Reiki energy flowing into your crown.

No need to place your hands anywhere. Simply receive while your body is completely still.

Bathe in this Light for a long time. Sit until you feel utterly peaceful.

Now, ask yourself the question: *Who am I?*

CHAPTER 13

BREATHING THROUGH LOSS

There are terrible moments in a human lifetime that take the breath away. Our lover dies. Our child goes missing. Fire. Volcano. Tornado. Car accident.

In these devastating moments, we feel the fragility of human life, and it brings us to tears.

In this intense, chaotic space, a full Reiki healing session may not be possible. Due to the swirl of emotion, we may not have the wherewithal to light a candle, play our favorite music, or rest on our favorite cushion. In this moment, the best we can hope for is to simply remember to breathe.

Practice Invitation

Reiki is not about 'doing it right.' The relationship we have with Reiki is not about following protocols, perfecting hand positions, or memorizing the wise words of our teacher. No. Reiki is, at core, about *allowing* the Universal Life Force Energy to move through us.

It is not that complicated.

Although I would never wish this fate for you, there may come a time, at some point on your journey (whether this lifetime or a future one), when you may feel completely overwhelmed. Your vision may be blurry; tears may sting. You may forget your name or forget the year. Your legs may shake like jelly. But, here's the good news…If this kind of moment happens to you, you'll remember this mantra:

Peace is the breath.

I am safe in the breath.

CHAPTER 14

THE FLOW OF SELF-HEALING

Some Reiki teachers recommend a fixed schedule for practicing self-healing sessions. They may even say that you must devote a particular number of minutes or hours every day.

However, what I have discovered is that a stringent approach to self-healing sessions is often counterproductive. What works better for most practitioners is a relaxed, free-flowing approach. There are a few reasons for this.

The first reason is that many of us Reiki practitioners have other beloved spiritual practices and traditions that are also dear to our hearts. In this era, rare are the souls who strictly devote one hundred percent of their waking efforts to any one path or tradition. Now, the norm on this burgeoning New Earth is that we are, most of us, quite eclectic, incorporating a variety of diverse healing tools into our kit. (There will always be a few rare beings who devote themselves fully and totally to one single path. These beings are the lineage bearers:

it's their mission to dive deeply into one tradition in order to pass along its pure essence throughout the ages.)

For most of us, as we spiritually awaken, we will embrace hybridization. We will integrate. We will mix and match. We will be wonderfully eclectic—without guilt or shame! Rarely will we consider ourselves the follower of a single teacher, let alone a single way! This is because New Earth is all about listening to the heart, about following our curiosity.

We can be dedicated Reiki practitioners while also rolling out our yoga mat. We can be Reiki teachers while also chanting magic spells under full moons. We can be one hundred percent committed to the path of Reiki while singing divine love songs to our Lord in the church choir. We can do it all. In this age, we have the blessing to clearly see Divinity in *all* practices, tools, paths, and methods of awakening.

The second reason that I usually do not recommend a strict schedule for practicing self-healing is this: The essence of the Reiki session is all about *rest*. It's about relaxation and non-doing. It's about surrender.

When we remember that the ultimate aim of our Reiki practice is to dissolve into the Christ Light, to dissolve into the Pure Love of Krishna, to dissolve into our Buddha Nature (the mystic essence that *all* religions point to, no matter the words we use to describe it), then we will truly understand how to approach our own healing. The most profound purpose of the Reiki hands-on healing session is, in truth, *not* actually about physical healing at all! It's *not* about perfecting the body or manifesting wealth or creating a comfortable worldly existence! What we are really here to do, at the deepest level, is to Wake Up. What we are here to do is *not* to seek temporary pleasures or acquire worldly desires…what we are here to do is discover liberation. In Sanskrit, this is known as *moksha*, or freedom from the illusion of separation.

It's the journey into Oneness.

Therefore, the best way to approach the precious gift of a Reiki self-healing session is to release control. True healing—realizing our inherent Oneness with all beings—naturally happens when we relinquish all notions of force, willpower, gain, success, and want. Instead, we relax. Instead, we trust. We listen. We chant our mantras and move our hands effortlessly. It's all happening *on its own*.

Of course, if you are a newcomer to the Reiki path *or* are a newcomer to spirituality in general, it is very beneficial to set yourself a daily goal for doing self-healing sessions. In the practice suggestions below, I'll share some specifics about how to do that. However, once that initial period of acclimatization has passed, it's great to take a more free-flowing approach to our self-healing sessions.

A Reiki self-healing session is meant to feel like falling into a warm, soft blanket. It's meant to be relaxing, a cozy break from the stressors of daily life. Ultimately, healing yourself with your hands is *not* meant to feel overly-challenging or like something that takes willpower or discipline. Instead, Reiki self-healing is a yummy-tasting medicine that we *want* to take. We look forward to it!! It's not something that we feel we 'must' do... rather, we learn to hear its tantalizing call. It's beckoning us with delight and relief. It's our coming Home.

After our introductory acclimatization period, if we simply allow our self-healing sessions to be spontaneous rather than planned, if we allow them to arise in the most-needed moments rather than something that we explicitly schedule, this is where the True Magic happens.

When we lovingly prepare our space—placing flowers on our altar, lighting a candle, playing heavenly music—we are inviting the Divine Mother to come and heal us. We are releasing control and meeting Her in a place of receptivity.

Whenever we feel a lack of peace and want to restore that peace, we know that Reiki self-healing is there for us.

Whenever we feel overwhelmed, lost, or wounded by the world, we have Reiki. It's our refuge. It's our angel. We can do it anytime, anywhere.

Having said all that, let me also be very clear: I am *not* saying that we shouldn't do Reiki self-healing sessions every day. We may very well end up doing that, due to the sheer joy and comfort that it brings us! What I *am* saying, however, is that it's important to drop the 'shoulds' and 'musts' when it comes to our self-healing journey. It's very vital to give ourselves absolute permission to go with the flow and to really tune into what's needed day-to-day.

After becoming a Reiki teacher, I spent the first few years under the illusion that I was somehow failing if I didn't spend at least one hour every day laying hands on myself. (This is what one of my trusted mentors had prescribed.) However, as the years passed, I started to realize that I was viewing the sacred ritual of Reiki self-healing in the wrong way. I realized that my rigidity was actually *detracting* from my ability to rest and heal. Eventually, after much contemplation, I experimentally released the rigid 'shoulds' and adopted a more organic approach. This was a vital turning point for me! I still spent hours every single day in spiritual practice (different forms of meditation, prayer, and yoga from various traditions), but I released the idea that I 'should' do hands-on healing every day. This freed up my energy tremendously and helped me to genuinely look forward to doing self-healing as a special treat.

So, what does my healing journey look like these days? Well, I really enjoy giving myself healing sessions before I go to sleep at night. Usually I will spend at least ten or twenty minutes relaxing on a far-infrared massage table while placing my hands wherever they are guided. (I don't set a timer for the session; I simply do it for however long feels good.) Sometimes I use crystals, sometimes I don't. Sometimes I use sage, sometimes I don't. Sometimes I chant Sanskrit mantras, sometimes I don't. Sometimes I invoke Krishna through prayer, sometimes I don't. Every night is different. It's all very intuitive and based upon my mood and what's going on in my life at the time.

A big part of why this evening routine works so well for me—why it has become such a consistent delight in my life—is because it's not something that I feel I 'should' do. It stays in the realm of spontaneity and flexible choice. This has made all the difference in the world!

Practice Invitation #1

If you are new to the path of Reiki and have not yet experienced a period of dedicated healing, please plan to do so. (Or, if you have been on this Reiki path for a long time, yet have not experienced a period of intensive healing, this invitation is for you, also.)

I recommend performing one hour-length healing session, every day, for at least twenty-one consecutive days. In addition, during these twenty-one days, perform Gassho meditation for at least twenty minutes as well as recite the precepts once in the morning and once in the evening. (I'll share more about Gassho in the next chapter.)

As you immerse yourself in the system of Reiki, take some time to journal about what you're discovering. Ponder the arts of self-healing and meditation. See if you can create some poetic, descriptive words to explain how Reiki is feeling to you. Some examples might be:

> *Reiki feels like stepping into a bath at the end of a long day.*
>
> *Reiki feels like sipping water after a long journey in the desert.*
>
> *Reiki feels like music after years of silence.*
>
> *Reiki feels like love.*

Practice Invitation #2

After you complete this twenty-one-day period, I recommend that you then set yourself free to let Reiki flow how it wants to flow. (If, at any point in the future, you're needing a reboot into the system of Reiki, feel free to return to this more intensive twenty-one-day practice schedule as needed.)

Every day, tune into what you truly want and need. Be honest with yourself! If what you want is a Reiki self-healing session, great! If what you want is to sit peacefully in Gassho, great! If what you want on a particular day is a spiritual practice from a different tradition, great! If you feel like exploring Reiki—but in a different, Divinely-inspired way, then please get creative! For example, during a stressful meeting at work, you may suddenly feel the urge to lay hands upon yourself (discretely on your thighs). Or, you may suddenly find yourself chanting the precepts during a traffic jam. Or, you may suddenly find yourself speaking Light-filled words to your plants while gardening. Let it all come to you. Be surprised at how it all seamlessly integrates into your life.

Give yourself permission to focus on other spiritual practices if that's what you truly want and need. For example, if your mind feels strong today, but your body feels weak, maybe rolling out your yoga mat would be best. Or, perhaps you feel such a deep love in your heart today that you desire to spend the whole day in *seva* (selfless service) out in the community. If that is what you truly want—do it!

In summary, I invite you to experiment with spontaneity. See what happens when you allow your self-healing sessions, as well as your other Reiki-related practices, to arise naturally, based on genuine desire. Having said that, though, if you are new to spirituality and do not yet already have a cornucopia of trusted practices that you regularly turn to, then I *do* recommend that you dedicate yourself to practicing at least one tool from the Reiki system every single day. Whether that means singing the precepts, sharing hands-on healings with other souls, visualizing the symbols, giving distance healing to our whole world, chanting mantras to bless your food, offering prayers of gratitude to teachers in your lineage, sitting quietly in Gassho meditation, or practicing some other technique that you learned in your Reiki training, it's good to get into the habit of doing at least one Reiki-related activity per day. In other words, while, in general, I do advocate a more flexible, free-flowing approach, we *do* need some amount of daily discipline in order to evolve. If we let even a few days go by without any spiritual practice at all, then it's easy to fall back into old patterns that may not support our growth.

Dear friend, the ultimate point I'm making is this: *Do at least one spiritual practice every day.* It doesn't have to be Reiki, although it could be. Here on this New Earth, we are no longer constrained by the dogmas that dictate that we should be true to only one path. Relax and have fun exploring this Magical Creation!

CHAPTER 15

GASSHO AS TRUE SELF

Rather than heal the body,
heal the mind.
When the mind is at peace,
the body is at ease.
When body and mind are both free,
the dragon roars in the withered tree.

DOGEN

The aim of all spiritual practice is to, eventually, transcend the very notion of 'practice' itself.

We practice love so that we can walk in love.

We practice kindness so that we can emanate kindness.

We practice peace so that we can be peace.

Eventually, we see that all of our methods, tools, and techniques are limited. They can only take us so far.

To continue our evolution, we must ultimately let go.

Gradually, gradually, the one who thinks she is practicing realizes her True Self.

Gradually, gradually, the one who thinks he is practicing realizes his True Self.

All our practices are meant to go deeper and deeper until eventually there is no measurement at all—there is only Being.

One such practice that has the potential to take us into the depths of Being is Gassho meditation.

It will begin as just a practice—*until something else happens.*

During our Level One Reiki training, many of us learn the beginner's form of Gassho: Seated upright, eyes closed, hands pressed together in prayer position in front of the heart, and mind focused solely on the sensations of the two middle fingers touching.

There are many wonderful aspects to this introductory phase of the practice. First, on an energetic level, Gassho grants us greater sensitivity. The more we are tuned into the sensation of our hands, the more we can sense energy. And the more we can sense energy, the better our ability to use our hands to help others heal.

Secondly, a benefit of our beginning practice is greater mental focus and clarity. In this day and age, many of us suffer from ADD and other attention-related challenges. By bringing awareness back to the body—in this case, the two middle fingers touching—we are given a precious medicine that grounds us back into the Wonderful Present Moment.

Finally, Gassho works on a symbolic level, helping to bring us back into balance. As the two hands come together, one hand symbolizes heaven and the other hand symbolizes Earth. Therefore, the practice is symbolic of a powerful process of *integration*: We are a Soul from the heavenly realms who is here to have a physical human experience here upon Earth.

Yes, this introductory way of practicing Gassho is very beautiful indeed. *And, also,* I invite you to go deeper.

Practice Invitation

Begin by sitting in traditional/beginner's Gassho (as I've just described). Sit in this way for as long as it takes to settle the body-mind. Depending on how your day is going, this may take five minutes or fifty minutes or longer. Give yourself plenty of space.

Eventually, a moment will arise naturally when you feel ready to advance to the next step. Note: Please do not rush or force the next step. Be gentle with yourself. There may be some days (stressful days) when what you need most is simply to sit in beginner's Gassho. This is perfectly okay.

The next step is to gently release the focus on your fingers. Rest your hands—with middle fingers still touching—down onto your lap.

Simply sit. Simply BE.

Allow your awareness to be pure. You're not clinging to anything. You're not focusing. You're simply sitting as Presence, as Being.

You now have no body, no form, no identity, no thoughts. This blessed space is what the Buddhists call śūnyatā (emptiness).

Sit in this blessed space for as long as naturally happens. Some days you will be blessed by śūnyatā for only a second or two; on other days, you will be able to dwell here for longer. Each day will be different.

Whenever you notice that your mind has again become active (reflecting on the past, planning for the future, pondering a question, etc.), return to the basic concentration of your two middle fingers touching. Consider these fingers as your safe haven, your home base.

Stay here with the middle fingers for as long as you need to. Then, a moment will perhaps again arise when you're ready to release again into emptiness.

Spend the rest of your meditation in a flowing alternation between attention on the fingers and the relaxation of letting go.

Allow the flow to be unforced and effortless.

As you work with this higher level of Gassho practice, it's important that you do not judge yourself when you catch your mind thinking and need to return again to the grounding point of your fingers. And don't criticize yourself when śūnyatā does not appear on a particular day, or if it only appears for a few seconds. Everything that happens during your meditation is perfect.

CHAPTER 16

EMBRACING
SENSATION

Slowly but surely,
you will become such an ally
for your own evolving journey
that the fear of the unknown
will transform into an excitement
to go where your awareness
has never gone before.

MATT KAHN

After many years of healing and reflection, I can now see how the illness and pain that I endured as a child was the absolute perfect scenario for me. It made me into a spiritual warrior. It woke me up and helped me to see the world with wide, compassionate eyes.

My story is the story of moving from self-hate to self-love. As a child, I coped with the chaos of my environment by blaming myself every time I got sick. Rather than entertaining the possibility that my illnesses were actually the physical manifestations of abuse, I began to hate myself. I berated myself with the same harsh words that were spoken to me by my society, by my overly-strict religious teachers, and by my caregivers. The possibility that I was being mistreated was simply too difficult of a concept for my child-brain to handle. On an unconscious level, I excused the adults' behavior and pointed the finger of blame back at myself—believing that there *had* to be some kind of cause for all this suffering.

Later, after becoming a Reiki healer, I noticed that every time the smallest symptom would arise—headache, stubbed toe, runny nose, etc.—a mean inner critic would suddenly emerge. This was the voice of my past. This was the voice of conditioned inner hatred. This voice would mock me, telling me that I was a failure. It would tell me that I was weak and that I was a lousy Reiki healer.

As I began to regularly witness these uncomfortable physical symptoms as well as these dark inner voices, a calm stillness descended upon my soul. I realized that none of what had happened to me was my fault. And, what's more, there was nobody to blame at all! Everybody was doing the absolute best that they could at the time. I began to have pre-birth memories, recalling in vivid detail how I *chose* to leave the angelic realms in order to take form upon Earth. I remembered *choosing* my parents, my birthplace, and the details of my life. All of these things were perfectly orchestrated *by me* (my higher self) so that my soul had the necessary karmic environment in which to purify, grow, and become enlightened.

I realized that nobody was to blame.

Nobody was to blame.

∞

So, how do we handle physical discomfort?

What is our relationship with pain?

As we grow into the role of a healer, we may get confused sometimes. We may feel that illness is 'bad.' We may view the natural decay of the body (old age) as something fundamentally wrong, as something that we must—at all costs—strive to defeat.

But… is this really the deepest way of seeing?

As we hear countless testimonials of miraculous Reiki healings, as we discover more and more scientific articles that demonstrate the effectiveness of energy healing, as we immerse ourselves within conscious community here on this blessed New Earth…we may get the false impression that it's our job to eradicate death and illness. And we may believe that it's our job to wage war against all unpleasant sensation.

But… is this really the truest way of seeing?

∞

If, like a pendulum, we swing wildly toward the side of believing that it is our mission to eradicate all bodily discomfort—waging war with disease and death like they're the enemy—then we will be left feeling exhausted and frustrated. We will be fighting a battle we can't win.

Being human means occupying a fallible body that will one day die. This is inevitable. The key, then, is to *die before we die*—to surrender the ego peacefully and accept the impermanence of form. This means that even the most serious illness or bodily discomfort need not cause us mental suffering. We can breathe and relax into the way things are.

At the same time, however, let us not be overly passive and unconsciously fall into a victim role. We *can* actively work to heal, change, and perhaps even cure certain chronic or terminal illnesses. Transformation is likely through a change in diet/lifestyle, daily Reiki healing, regular meditation, and simply the peace of mind that comes through living the precepts.

So, as you can see, it's about finding balance. The desire to heal bodily pains is a perfectly beautiful spiritual impulse! And, at the very same time, let us pursue this aim in a cautious, humble, open-hearted way that does not attach to specific outcomes.

Let us do our healing work and then let go.

Let us do our healing work and trust that God knows what's best.

In other words, let us work diligently to do whatever we can to strengthen our bodies *while simultaneously* bowing to the Big Mind that knows how all the puzzle pieces best fit together.

Yes, it's absolutely empowering and wonderful to watch our illnesses dissolve. Yes, it's absolutely thrilling to watch our deepest dreams manifest into form—but let us not get caught up in stories about 'what should be' or 'what I deserve.' Let us simply witness the unfolding with reverence.

Indeed, our role as Reiki practitioners is very, very simple. We devote our lives to Being the Light. We practice diligently. We take time for stillness. We move past plateaus and rise beyond plaguing doubts. We keep going. We keep moving. We stop; we move again. We observe. We breathe. We create space within us that watches all things, unattached to fulfillment of any particular dreams.

We work and we wait.

We speak and we listen.

Ultimately, we surrender to the Infinite Love of God in our Heart. We open our minds to Not Knowing—which, ironically, is the surest path to Peace!

In some scenarios, people will *need* pain as their teacher. The pain will drive them inward. In other scenarios, the approaching shadow of death will be a blessed breakthrough to fully appreciating the light of life.

In other words, what sometimes appears as 'bad' is actually a huge spiritual boon!

Remembering the fifth precept helps. To have compassion for ourselves and others means that we have compassion not just for people, but for *everything that happens*. We extend our compassionate arm to even the pain, death, and illnesses of this world. *Everything*.

Practice Invitation #1

Relax comfortably in an area of your home that feels safe and cozy. This could be your bed or favorite chair.

Once you're settled in, spend at least ten minutes witnessing each physical sensation as it arises.

Do not judge any of the sensations as good or bad. Do not attach any praise or blame. Simply observe.

The goal of this practice is simply to watch. You are *not* trying to make these sensations go away. You are learning to perceive these sensations detached from emotion; you are witnessing them as purely energetic phenomena, as neutral events that rise and fall in the Universe.

Practice Invitation #2

Once you have become familiar with witnessing sensations, it's time to go deeper. It's time to *embrace* the sensations.

The next time you are dealing with physical illness or bodily discomfort, make the choice to say *yes* to them. Make the choice to energetically *step into these sensations*. You can do this by visualizing that these sensations are a color and that you are absorbing this color into your skin. Or, you may simply hold the intention that these sensations are welcome.

These sensations are your portal, your doorway into a higher state of Consciousness. They are your teacher.

Whatever you feel—whether that be throbbing, aching, burning, numbness, itching, piercing, or fatigue—courageously say *yes* to it all. Be a willing receiver of what the Universe wants to show you.

Listen and stay alert for the presence of inner voices. Are there voices telling you that you can't do this practice or that it's too hard? Are there any voices of blame or shame?

If you listen carefully, you may hear things like:

"You're pathetic. Why can't you get it together?"

"You're weak and stupid."

"You're always making messes with your life!"

"Nobody loves you."

"You'll be alone forever."

"This pain is never gonna stop."

"God is punishing me."

"I must be a bad person."

As you practice embracing sensation, listen for what's being spoken in your inner world. If you notice any mean-spirited voices, take a breath, and call to mind the *Choku Rei*. Draw it or chant it. Remind yourself that you are a perfect, whole, and complete being—just as you are. Remind yourself that this physical issue is not your fault.

As you sit with this symbol, allow its energy to permeate your Being. All is indeed well; there is not a hair out of place in God's Universe. *These physical sensations are here to teach you greater levels of peace and acceptance.* In the same way that a mountain climber embraces the most difficult peaks in order to stretch her capacity for bravery, you are being gifted a precious opportunity. You are invited to discover the calm within the storm. This is a skill that eventually you will master and share with others.

CHAPTER 17

THE BLESSING OF JŌSHIN KOKYŪ HŌ

Jōshin Kokyū Hō is a simple yet profound breathing practice that purifies mind and heart. It helps us to find peaceful center in times of difficulty and helps us to forge respectful, creative, expansive relationships based upon the true knowledge of how the Universe works.

If we are experiencing intense arguments, communication blockages, and frequent upsets in our personal interactions, it's because we are (temporarily) lost in the swirl of ego. In such a swirl, the mind is convinced that what we need to do is to defend, attack, protect, or hide. It's all about *me-me-me*. In this tense state, our hearts close and we cannot truly connect.

As the building of New Earth is of course a group project, it's imperative for us to embody the fifth precept as much as possible. (Please see Chapter 5 for more about this precept.) We do this by detaching ourselves from self-centeredness and self-righteousness. Through the regular practice of Jōshin Kokyū Hō, we build our compassion muscle and loosen the warlike grip of ego.

And what is the ego, you ask? Well, the ego is simply a child of time. It's the mistaken belief that we are a separate entity who must fight to survive; it's the mistaken belief that death is real and that the clock is winding down. It's forgetting we are an Eternal Soul.

Conflict in relationships can only happen when we are stuck in time, stuck in the fearful ego…

When we forget who we truly are, we fight.

When we feel we have something to lose, we judge.

And when we don't feel our cosmic connection to the Universe, we disconnect from each other.

Indeed, whenever we are dwelling in the past (holding grudges or nostalgically reminiscing) or racing toward the future (worrying or over-planning), we are forgetting our True Identity—which is a Limitless Being of Light. This Being of Light is the True Self, the one who lives outside of time, the one who (ultimately) has no boundaries and has nothing to fight against or protect.

The Reiki meditation technique Jōshin Kokyū Hō is a miraculous opportunity to break free from false beliefs. It expands our energetic awareness and helps us to connect with others and Self in a peaceful—and even blissful!—way. It brings us out of the swirl of ego and back into the glorious present moment: the only place where we find true harmony.

Practice Invitation

The next time you're experiencing anxiety, strife, or confusion in a relationship, take some time to perform Jōshin Kokyū Hō. Or, better yet, practice this technique daily as a preventative medicine.

This practice has three main steps. The first step is to bring the Reiki healing energy into your body—to cultivate self-awareness and self-love. The second step is to use the energy to heal your auric field and disconnect from limiting thought patterns. The final step is to send the beautiful healing energy out into the planet and the whole Universe.

The following is a more detailed description of each step.

Step One:

Perform this meditation seated upright with eyes closed. I recommend *not* setting a timer for this meditation: give yourself plenty of space to go with the flow; take as long as you need.

Inhale Reiki energy into your crown chakra (located at the top of your head). Continue to inhale, bringing that energy all the way down into your sacral chakra (an inch or two below your belly button). On the exhale, visualize the energy radiating out from your sacral into every part of your body. See the energy swirl down your legs and travel up your chest and into your arms. See every part of your body radiating with this beautiful healing energy. Watch and witness this miracle for as long as feels good.

Step Two:

Now it's time to clear your aura and release any negative energetic attachments.

Repeat the same kind of inhale from the first step: breathe energy into your crown and then bring that energy all the way down into your sacral. This time, however, use a different intention for your exhalations. When you breathe out, spread the Reiki energy outward to fill your aura. (The aura is an egg-shaped energy field that surrounds your physical form, typically extending outward at least a few feet around your body). On every exhalation, visualize that the Light of Reiki is completely filling and cleansing your aura. If you sense any blockages, old energy cords, or karmic residue, allow these to be dissolved back into the Light. (There is no need to fear blockages, cords, or karmic residues: these are simply outdated, toxic thought patterns that your heart is ready to release.)

It can be helpful to do this cleaning work in sections. First, clean the top part of your aura (over your head); then do the bottom (under your feet); then work on the left/right; and finally finish the process by focusing on front/back. After you've thoroughly cleaned each section, pour Reiki healing energy into all of your aura simultaneously. Watch your whole being glow.

Step Three:

You are now ready to direct the Reiki energy out into New Earth as well as the whole Universe!

After you've thoroughly immersed yourself in the first and second steps, you'll know—spontaneously and effortlessly—when you're ready to move to this final step.

When you're ready, simply visualize the Reiki energy flowing into your crown, down into your sacral, and then shoot it outward to fill the whole planet. See all the plants, animals, rivers, nations, and beings everywhere healed by this Light. Take a few moments to send this Light to any human(s) with whom you've been having relational difficulty. Finally, send Reiki out into the entire Universe! See all the planets, stars, suns, moons, and galaxies radiating with this Light.

Step Four:

To close this meditation, bring your palms together in prayer position. Give gratitude and thank the Universe that you're able to perform this meditation. Count your blessings and remember how miraculous this particular lifetime truly is!

CHAPTER 18

RELEASING KARMA, FORGIVING DARKNESS

Compassion is the purpose
of our True Self.

FRANS STIENE

Let's talk about something that nobody wants to talk about.

Let's talk about the darkness.

Sometimes it happens that, while we're laying our light-filled hands upon someone, we suddenly feel a wave of fear. Or sometimes it happens that, while we're holding space for another, a dark thought suddenly pops into our mind. The thought may range from slightly irritating to intensely grotesque. We might see, hear, or sense a murder, rape, battle, torture, or some other horrific event happening. We might even see ourselves as the perpetrator!

Whenever we have an experience like this during a Reiki session, it can be so, so confusing.

First, it's important not to panic. If this happens to you, please remember that this is a very common experience for Reiki practitioners. So know that you are not alone.

Second, this is a time for mindfulness. This is a time to stay present and breathe. It's important not to react to those dark thoughts with judgment, fear, or aversion. In other words, it's important not to layer the dark thought with another dark thought. Such a burden is not necessary.

In all actuality, the dark thought is a blessing—if we choose to view it that way. The dark thought is simply a sign that old energy is being released, that old karma is being healed. The dark thought is a signal that a deeper healing is taking place—not only for the one being healed but also for the healer, too. Everyone is healing together.

Remember: Reiki is not always about rainbows and roses. Of course, it's the *promise* of rainbows and roses that initially draws us to the practice… however, as we progress upon the path, we need to learn the lesson of neutrality. Of witnessing. Of learning unperturbability. We need to know how to simply observe something without condemning it.

Ultimately, we Reiki healers are in cosmic training. We are learning to view everything that happens—EVERYTHING—as divinely purposeful. We are learning trust.

No matter how scary the thought, it's possible to witness and not react.

No matter how weird or strange the vision, we can still remain as Awareness.

In other lifetimes, we may have had a lot of difficulty with the person on our table. Maybe they killed us or we killed them. Or maybe the vision we're seeing is simply the unresolved trauma of some tragic event that has nothing to do with us. In any case, here upon this New Earth, we have the opportunity to re-write old scripts. *Hallelujah!!* By not judging, ancient karma is released. Everything is made new in the here and now.

Practice Invitation

If a dark thought arises while you share Reiki healing with someone, don't spend any time worrying about it. Don't try to analyze *why* the dark thought has arisen. Don't interpret. Simply take a few breaths and remember these words:

Everything is OK. There's healing happening. Ancient karma is being released.

Notice the relief that washes over your body as you remind yourself of these truths. Be grateful for the deep wisdom you carry as a Lightworker who is guided every step of the way.

And please know that if a few moments of fear happen before you remember these words, that's okay too! Know that you haven't hurt anybody; your channel has still been flowing the Reiki energy perfectly this whole time. You and they are protected.

After the session, if you choose to contemplate the possible meanings and reasons for the dark thought, you may choose to do so—but make sure to do it in a loving and self-compassionate way. However, it's important that, for the duration of the Reiki session itself, to not think about it. Don't spend any time in analysis: simply Breathe and Trust.

CHAPTER 19

DIVINE UNION

If you are yourself at peace,

then there is at least some peace in the world.

Then share your peace with everyone

and everyone will be at peace.

THOMAS MERTON

Just for today, do not worry.

What is the underlying meaning of this first Reiki precept?

It is the glorious permission to relax. To surrender.

And why is this important? To cease worry is to cease our limited sense of self. To cease worry is to become boundless. To cease worry is to merge with the All and surrender to Divine Will.

To cease worry is, ultimately, a humble request. *Make me an empty vessel, O God. Create in me a pure heart.*

∞

One of the most beautiful aspects of a Reiki healing session is that the giver (the one facilitating the session) offers the gift of bodily comfort. They ask questions to help bring ease: *Would you like some tea? What about an extra blanket? Do you like the temperature in the room?* The giver is also keenly aware of the body language of the receiver, doing their best to tune into any unspoken needs.

Sometimes the receiver needs a little extra help in relaxing, so the giver may suggest a meditative practice or explain a few breathing tips to begin the session. But make no mistake: *There is no duality happening here.* As the giver teaches, they are being taught. As the giver speaks, they also hear.

Yes, this is a Divine moment of collapsing duality. As the session progresses, the giver is feeling the physical sensations within their own body, which mirror what the receiver is feeling. Thus, the giver knows exactly where to place their hands.

There are not two bodies anymore—only One.

The giver opens up their spiritual eyes and ears to receive the messages that come from Spirit. Again, no duality here. The messages shared not only help the receiver, but benefit the giver too, by helping to cement previous lessons. No duality: Everyone is healing together.

Thus, we can view the Reiki hands-on healing session as a profound gateway to Unity. As the giver enters a meditative, open state of channeling, their grasp on the well-guarded sense of I/me/mine dissolves. They release their sense of being a separate individual. This release then translates into the compassionate way that the giver touches and speaks—for they are truly touching *their own body*; they are truly speaking *to their own heart*.

For the receiver, as they experience the miracle of being touched in the most perfect, soothing way, their heart is inextricably filled with love. There's no longer two hearts: There's One.

Practice Invitation #1

The Reiki healing session is nothing less than the gift of two mortals transcending their limitation of form. It is Divine Union. It's peace and, often, bliss.

The next time you're in the process of sharing a healing session, notice the thoughts you're thinking. Are you second-guessing yourself or doubting the Miracle of what's happening? Is there any underlying anxiety? Are you worrying about outcomes? Be aware of every thought that passes through your mind. Observe.

If you become aware of any thoughts that are less than total trust in the Universe, do not despair! Simply comfort your mind with the first precept as well as some gentle, nurturing reassurances.

My dear dear mind,

I love you.

I promise, everything's going to be okay.

Just for today, you don't have to worry. You can relax.

Everything is happening perfectly.

After sharing these words, simply witness your hands as they move or are still. Don't analyze what the hands are doing. Simply watch. Don't think about the chakras; don't think about the receiver's diagnosis; don't think about 'results.' Simply allow your body and hands to move—or not move—with a quiet, open, spacious mind.

Practice Invitation #2

The next time you are sharing Reiki healing with another soul, help them feel that they are safe and unconditionally loved. Help them feel that they don't have to 'do' anything to be worthy of healing.

After you have guided them in some initial breathwork or guided meditation (just to help them calm and center for the first few moments of lying on the table), take a few minutes to whisper some peaceful words to them:

You can rest now, my dear.

You don't have to meditate or breathe in any certain way now. You don't have to make anything happen.

It's time to rest.

Let your mind do whatever it wants to do.

Let your body move if it wants to move, or let it be still.

Thoughts may come and go—that's wonderful.

You may even fall asleep—that's wonderful too!

This is your time. Please relax.

I'm here with you and I love you.

Practice Invitation #3

It's wonderful to include a brief gratitude ritual at the conclusion of every Reiki healing session.

After you release your hands from the receiver's body, slowly back away a few feet and bow reverently. (Or, if you're doing a remote healing session, simply bow in your mind's eye.)

When you bow, telepathically send the message: "Thank you, dear soul, for playing the role of the receiver today. I'm so grateful to have played the role of giver. May we both be blessed."

As you offer these heartfelt words, imagine that these words are traveling directly from your heart to their heart.

Finally, imagine these two hearts merging into One Big Heart. All is love and peace.

CHAPTER 20

NO MASTER

To see yourself in everyone

and to realize

that everyone is in you

is the supreme aim of spiritual knowledge.

ANANDAMAYI MA

In the East, honorary titles such as *Sensei, Rinpoche, Guru, Babaji,* or *Maharishi* are given to teachers who possess a high level of spiritual attainment. These terms are usually bestowed upon a teacher after many, many intense (and usually grueling) years of training. They are titles given by others; rarely are they used in self-reference. This is because, in the East, it is widely understood that the spiritual teacher is a servant (not a master) of others. Humility IS the path.

As we dive deeper into our beloved Reiki practice, we will naturally grow more and more humble and become more and more mindful of the words that we use to describe ourselves. We are mindful of this because we realize that every single human being is God. We realize that ALL are Divinity.

Everyone is Buddha.

Practice Invitation

Ponder the following questions. Through deep introspection, discover if you are using the most aligned language to convey the non-hierarchical/nondual version of New Earth you wish to co-create.

Through these questions, dig deep into some of the underlying views you have about your human relationships. (If some of these questions do not apply to your journey at this time, please skip them.) I recommend writing your responses in a journal or creating an audio/video recording so as to shed greater light on your ideal visions.

- What is the most rewarding or joyful aspect of my service to New Earth?
- When I'm offering hands-on healing to another person, how often am I thinking of myself as a "Reiki practitioner" or "Reiki Master" or "business owner" or "healer"? Am I overly attached to these labels?
- Do I withhold compassion and love from any particular group of people or certain individuals?
- How would I, ideally, like to relate to everyone?
- Do I refer to the people who share money for Reiki sessions as "clients"? How might my heart feel if, instead, I thought of them as friends, loves, sisters, brothers, souls, tribe, or family?
- When I'm working with a Soul who's going through a difficult time, do words such as "broken" or "sick" ever enter my

mind? Do I feel that people need to be fixed? Do I feel that I have the answers that people need?

- Do I trust that every Soul has full competency to hear their inner guru?
- Am I cultivating all of my human relationships in the spirit of equality?
- When I am creating and sharing marketing materials online, what labels am I using to describe myself and the gifts that flow through me? Do these labels align with the values of humility and Oneness?

CHAPTER 21

PORTRAIT OF A NEW EARTH

The gravitational pull that our own being exerts
on its own apparently contracted, limited form
is referred to as grace.
As such, grace is not a special moment
that is conferred upon us by some external deity.
It is the continuous attraction of our deepest self,
inviting us to return home
to the peace of our being.

RUPERT SPIRA

Once upon a time, in a time outside of time, there is a human being standing tall atop a hill. That human being is smiling. That human being is You.

Maybe this You lives later in this lifetime, or maybe this is a You who is living a future lifetime. In truth, it really doesn't matter. Though the outward form may have changed, it is still You. The continuation of your essence.

This is the story of You.

∞

The sun shines. A few white puffy clouds celebrate a vast, open blue. Blue, blue, blue everywhere.

In your heart, there is peace. You hum a few happy tunes to yourself.

A sudden wind arises, and you remove your scarf so as to feel the deliciousness on your skin. You pause in your humming for a moment to reflect with gratitude.

You are here on this hill today to be with her again, your beloved Reiki teacher. Even though her body is now ashes, you feel her Presence even more strongly than when she lived in form.

You are here today to remember her.

You gently kneel down upon beloved Gaia. The tears are coming fast, but there's a new quality to them now, a different feeling. The grieving process is nearly complete.

As you allow these precious tears to slip down your cheeks, you reflect upon the goodness of life: the ease with which your children have understood the system of Reiki and how schools on every street corner now include meditation, yoga, and other healing arts within their curriculum.

Yes, today is a day for gratitude! Placing your palms together in *Gassho*, kneeling upon the soft soft grass, you survey the vista below. This is your beloved village. A few hundred people gathered together to uplift one another. You're glad that nobody lives in big cities anymore. Thank goodness those dark days are done! What's here now is such abundance: every household growing their own food, rivers and waters returning to pristine elegance, children playing unsupervised in nearby forests.

Releasing your body now, laying directly upon the Earth, you place your right cheek against the soft mix of grass and soil.

Breathing in, Breathing out

Breathing in, Breathing out

Awareness upon the Heart

You reflect with gratitude upon the final attunement she gave you, a few days prior to leaving her body. Such a blessed *reiju*. Her yellow curtains blowing in the early spring wind. Even though she was very ill, she somehow still managed to prepare the tea so beautifully. She was always serving.

Raising your head up now from warm Mother Earth, resting your chin upon your palms, the third Reiki symbol now comes vividly into your mind, spontaneously bursting into a cornucopia of blues and purples. You love how the colors seem to arrive of their own accord. No planning needed.

Your teacher's voice rings in your ear now, sounding like the clearest, most comforting bell:

In the beginning of the journey, my dear child, you believed that you were drawing energy into you. You believed that the special thing you needed was outside of you. But now you know the Truth... that you ARE that energy, you ARE that Love. You have always been That. And there is nothing to reach for, nothing to attain. Our job is simply to remember.

That, my child, is the Truth. That, my child, is the Way.